DINING AND DWELLING

Dining and Dwelling

Proceedings of a public seminar on archaeological discoveries
on national road schemes, August 2008

Edited by Michael Stanley, Ed Danaher and James Eogan

NRA
An tÚdarás um Bóithre Náisiúnta
National Roads Authority

Published by the National Roads Authority 2009
St Martin's House
Waterloo Road
Dublin 4

Cover illustrations

Main image:
Still from a 3D-animated reconstruction of a medieval moated site excavated at Ballinvinny South, Co. Cork, on the N8 Glanmire–Watergrasshill road scheme (Digitale Archäologie).

Smaller pictures (from left to right):
The baseplates of the wheel-pit and flume of a spectacularly well-preserved early medieval wooden watermill excavated at Kilbegly, Co. Roscommon, on the N6 Athlone–Ballinasloe road scheme (Valerie J Keeley Ltd).
Six-row hulled barley (left), emmer wheat (middle) and two-row hulled barley (right), the first plants to be cultivated in Ireland during the Neolithic period (Meriel McClatchie).
Billy Quinn heating water in a trough with fired rocks during an experiment to test whether some Bronze Age fulachta fiadh*/burnt mounds were used as micro-breweries* (Moore Group).

Cover design: Wordwell Ltd

ISBN 978-0-9545955-7-9
ISSN 1649-3540

British Library Cataloguing-in-Publication Data.
A catalogue record for this book is available from the British Library.

First published in 2009

Typeset in Ireland by Wordwell Ltd

Printed by Castuera, Pamplona

Contents

Foreword

Dining and Dwelling is the sixth monograph to be published in this series by the National Roads Authority (NRA) and presents the proceedings of the NRA National Archaeology Seminar held at the Gresham Hotel, Dublin, on 28 August 2008 as part of National Heritage Week. This popular annual seminar series, which caters specifically for a non-specialist audience, showcases the diversity of archaeological discoveries made on national road schemes throughout Ireland in recent years. In common with the most recent seminars in the series, the 2008 event focused on a particular theme—dining and dwelling, addressing the archaeological evidence for food production, processing and consumption and rural settlement in Ireland from the earliest farmers through to the 19th century. The authors, who include archaeologists, archaeobotanists and zooarchaeologists, describe a wealth of previously unknown archaeological remains uncovered in counties Carlow, Cork, Galway, Kildare, Kilkenny, Limerick, Offaly, Roscommon and Tipperary on new sections of the N6, N7, N8, N9/N10 and N17 routes.

Highlights from *Dining and Dwelling* include the excavation of a spectacularly well-preserved early medieval wooden watermill at Kilbegly, Co. Roscommon; an account of the use of experimental archaeology to examine the theory that some Bronze Age *fulachta fiadh*/burnt mounds (ubiquitous on Irish road schemes) were actually micro-breweries; an examination of early medieval feasting as evidenced by an exquisite zoomorphic, or animal-like, drinking-horn terminal mount of copper alloy recovered during excavations at Ballyvass, Co. Kildare; and a consideration of the challenges and opportunities presented by the use of advanced computer technology and visualisation software to create 3D-animated reconstructions of ancient dwellings.

The contributors to the present volume are to be congratulated on producing papers that amply fulfil the promise of their fine presentations delivered only 12 months ago. While the NRA is very proud of its continuing achievements in successfully bringing the proceedings to publication on the anniversary of the seminar, this would not be possible without the expertise and hard work of the staff of the many archaeological consultancies and academic institutions that contribute to the national roads-building programme. I am very pleased to be able to acknowledge and pay tribute to this successful partnership, and trust that such fruitful cooperation will develop and flourish further in the years ahead, capitalising on the considerable investment that the NRA has made with regard to archaeological investigations by deepening our understanding of Ireland's rich heritage and disseminating the results to the widest possible audience.

Fred Barry
Chief Executive
National Roads Authority

Acknowledgements

The NRA would like to express its appreciation to Philip Barratt, Amy Bogaard, Michelle Delaney, Tara Doyle, Colm Flynn, Ken Hanley, Neil Jackman, Richard Jennings, Penny Johnston, Alison Kyle, Patricia Long, Gillian McCarthy, Meriel McClatchie, Melanie McQuade, Declan Moore, Colm Moriarty, TJ O'Connell, Nial O'Neill, Jerry O'Sullivan, Billy Quinn, Rick Schulting, Angus Stephenson, Karen Stewart, John Tierney, Auli Tourunen and Nicki Whitehouse for their contributions to the seminar and proceedings. The 2008 seminar was organised by Lillian Butler, Senior Administrator, Michael Stanley, Archaeologist, and Frantisek Zak Matyasowszky, Assistant Archaeologist, NRA. Bernadette Denning and Anneliese Jones, NRA, also assisted in the organisation of the seminar, and Sébastien Joubert, NRA Senior Archaeologist (acting), and Michael MacDonagh, NRA Senior Archaeologist, co-chaired the event.

Michael Stanley, Ed Danaher, NRA Archaeologist, and James Eogan, NRA Senior Archaeologist, prepared the proceedings for publication. The authors, Eachtra Archaeological Projects, Headland Archaeology Ltd, Irish Archaeological Consultancy Ltd, Margaret Gowen & Co. Ltd, Moore Group Ltd, Valerie J Keeley Ltd and the Ulster Museum all kindly supplied illustrations. The monograph was copy-edited by Emer Condit and was designed and typeset by Wordwell Ltd.

Material from Ordnance Survey Ireland is reproduced with the permission of the Government of Ireland and Ordnance Survey Ireland under permit number EN0045206.

Note on radiocarbon dates

All of the radiocarbon dates cited in the following papers are calibrated date ranges equivalent to the probable calendrical age of the sample and are expressed at the two-sigma (98% probability) level of confidence. Appendix 1 provides full details of all the available radiocarbon dates from the excavated archaeological sites described in these proceedings.

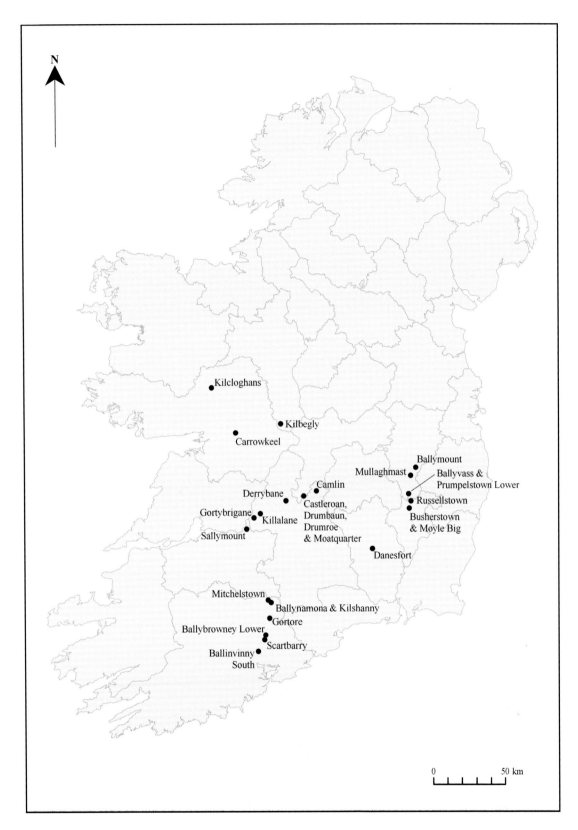

N

Kilcloghans

Kilbegly

Carrowkeel

Ballymount

Mullaghmast
Ballyvass &
Prumpelstown Lower

Camlin

Derrybane

Castleroan,
Drumbaun,
Drumroe
& Moatquarter

Russellstown

Gortybrigane
Killalane

Busherstown
& Moyle Big

Sallymount

Danesfort

Mitchelstown
Ballynamona & Kilshanny
Gortore

Ballybrowney Lower
Scartbarry

Ballinvinny
South

0   50 km

Locations of archaeological sites described in these proceedings.

1. Cultivating societies: new insights into agriculture in Neolithic Ireland

Meriel McClatchie, Nicki Whitehouse, Rick Schulting, Amy Bogaard and Philip Barratt

Illus. 1—When incorporated into a fire, plant components can become charred and survive in the archaeological record. Neolithic charred wheat grains from Kerloge, Co. Wexford, are shown on the left (Meriel McClatchie).

The earliest evidence for agriculture in Ireland has been dated to the Early Neolithic period, beginning around 4000 BC. From the outset of the Neolithic, previous food procurement strategies—including hunting, fishing and gathering—began to be replaced by plant and animal husbandry. Archaeological texts often mention the 'first farmers' when referring to the Neolithic period. While the main crops are known to have been wheat and barley, far less is known about the balance between them, the relative importance of different varieties within these crops, the methods used in crop production and the intensity of agricultural activity. This paper will examine the evidence for cereal cultivation in Neolithic Ireland—based upon archaeobotanical studies—and introduce a new research project that aims to investigate the timing, nature and effects of the introduction of agriculture into Ireland.

Archaeobotany and the preservation of ancient plants

Archaeobotany is the study of past societies and environments through the analysis of preserved plant remains, the remains usually being derived from archaeological deposits. A broad range of plant remains can be studied in archaeobotany, including seeds and fruits of higher plants, vegetative components of plants, parenchymatous tissues (underground storage organs of plants, such as roots and tubers), fibres, phytoliths (plant opal silica bodies), wood, pollen and starch granules, as well as lower plants, such as mosses and fungi. This paper will focus on non-wood plant macro-remains, such as cereal grains and chaff.

Fragmentary remains of plants can survive for thousands of years if subjected to certain processes. Many archaeological sites reveal traces of past fires. If plant components are incorporated into a fire and burnt when the supply of oxygen is insufficient for combustion to occur, they can become charred and survive in the archaeological record (Illus. 1). Charring is the most common method of plant preservation in Neolithic archaeological deposits, and can result from a range of actions, which may be accidental or purposeful. Accidental burning can occur when cereals are dried in the vicinity of a fire following a damp harvest, prior to storage, during the separation of grains from chaff or in association with malting. Accidental charring of plant components can also occur as a result of catastrophic fires, such as the burning of grain stores or house and roofing structures. Purposeful burning may result from actions such as the burning of an enemy's fields or stored crops, as well as the burning of stubble in fields and other traditional agricultural techniques. The burning of domestic waste—including floor sweepings and food debris—as fuel or simple rubbish disposal can also lead to the preservation of plant remains. Plants that are more likely to come into contact with fire during food processing, preparation and disposal activities—such as cereals, pulses, arable weeds and nutshells—often dominate assemblages of charred plant macro-remains.

Another method of preservation occurs when material is incorporated into anoxic conditions, whereby oxygen is excluded from deposits and plant tissues do not break down. Anoxic preservation is also referred to as waterlogging and anaerobic preservation, and can occur in areas with a high water-table, in deposits of a very organic nature, and occasionally when archaeological deposits are well sealed, for example by a heavy clay. Anoxic preservation is often encountered in natural deposits from environments such as peatlands, rivers and lakes. Relatively few Neolithic archaeological sites in Ireland have, however, produced waterlogged non-wood plant macro-remains.

Cereal types of Neolithic Ireland

The recovery of charred barley and wheat remains from Neolithic archaeological deposits indicates that these crops were the first plants to be cultivated in Ireland (Illus. 2). Barley spikelets (each spikelet contains a grain) are arranged in groups of three placed alternately along the stalk. In two-row barley only the middle spikelet in each group produces a ripe grain, and so the head appears to have two rows. In six-row barley all of the spikelets ripen. Two main varieties of two-row and six-row barley have been recorded in archaeological deposits in Ireland: hulled and naked. In the case of hulled barley, the husks (chaff) are actually fused onto the grains. With naked barley, the husks just enclose the grains rather than being fused—in this case the grain is more easily released from the chaff.

Illus. 2—Left: six-row hulled barley; middle: emmer wheat; right: two-row hulled barley (Meriel McClatchie).

50mm

Wheat also can be divided into hulled and naked varieties. Like barley, when wheat is hulled the husks are fused to the grain. With naked wheat the grain is more easily released. Hulled wheats—including emmer and spelt wheat—are rarely grown today and are often viewed as 'ancient' crop types. In recent years, however, spelt wheat has enjoyed something of a revival. Naked wheats—including bread wheat—are sometimes thought to be more modern than hulled wheats. It should, however, be noted that evidence for naked wheats has been recorded, albeit in small quantities, from Neolithic Ireland (for example Groenman van Waateringe 1984, 327), while substantial deposits of naked wheat were recorded at a Neolithic structure in Balbridie, Scotland (Fairweather & Ralston 1993).

Oat grains are occasionally found in Neolithic deposits, but are thought to represent arable weeds at this time rather than being cultivated in their own right. Cultivation of rye is also unlikely to have occurred until thousands of years later. Rye grains do not appear in the archaeological record in Ireland until the Middle Bronze Age (after 1700 BC), when they are also likely to have been arable weeds, perhaps not being cultivated until the historic period.

Where have the cereal remains been found?

The sampling of archaeological deposits for ancient cereal remains became more common in Ireland from the 1970s, and well over 100 Neolithic sites have been excavated since this time. While studies of the morphology and architectural arrangement of Neolithic structures and enclosures have been published (for example Grogan 2002; Smyth 2006), evidence for the cereal remains recovered from these sites has rarely been fully published and is not well understood. A recent study carried out by Jones and Rowley-Conwy (2007, 396) identified 10 Neolithic sites in Ireland where cereal remains have been found (Illus. 3). Although cereal remains have been recorded from many more sites, the evidence is not easily accessible, mainly owing to a lack of publication. As a result, Ireland is often conspicuously absent from discussions relating to the earliest farmers in Europe. Where Ireland is referred to in general European studies, it is often mentioned as an adjunct to Britain, thereby linking production and consumption practices between these two areas. This is despite the fact that the general archaeological evidence for the Neolithic differs in many respects between Ireland and Britain (Cooney 2000).

The cereal remains from an Early Neolithic rectangular house at Tankardstown South, Co. Limerick (Gowen 1988; Monk 1988), are often interpreted as representing a typical assemblage from Neolithic Ireland. At Tankardstown South hundreds of wheat remains—including grains and chaff fragments—were found. Where identifiable to species, the wheat remains are thought to represent emmer wheat. There is no definite evidence for barley at Tankardstown South. This site is very often drawn upon when we talk about the 'first farmers', but is it representative of crop cultivation throughout Neolithic Ireland? In order to test this hypothesis, McClatchie (forthcoming) carried out a brief review of cereal remains from Neolithic Ireland, which incorporated evidence from recently excavated sites that have not yet been published. This resulted in evidence of cereal remains from a total of 24 sites, a significant increase compared with previous studies. While wheat was predominant at many sites, barley (often the naked variety) was also recorded at more than half of all sites, suggesting more variation in the cereal types being used than was previously assumed. Furthermore, the presence of cereals at a substantial range of site types highlights the potential for gaining a better understanding of the different ways that foods may have been prepared and consumed in different situations.

A new research project on Neolithic agriculture in Ireland

McClatchie's study was presented at a conference in 2007 entitled *Living Landscapes: exploring Neolithic Ireland and its wider context*. The conference—which was held at Queen's University, Belfast, and sponsored by the NRA—brought together international researchers, including specialists in landscapes, plants, animals and other types of material remains, such as pottery. It highlighted a range of issues relating to early agriculture that needed further study, and a research project was formulated in order to address these issues. Commencing in June 2008 and entitled *Cultivating Societies: assessing the evidence for agriculture in Neolithic Ireland*, the project was funded by the Heritage Council under the 2008 Irish National Strategic Archaeological Research programme, or INSTAR. The project's main aim is to explore the timing, nature and effects of the introduction of agriculture in Ireland, and to compare this evidence with other areas in Europe.

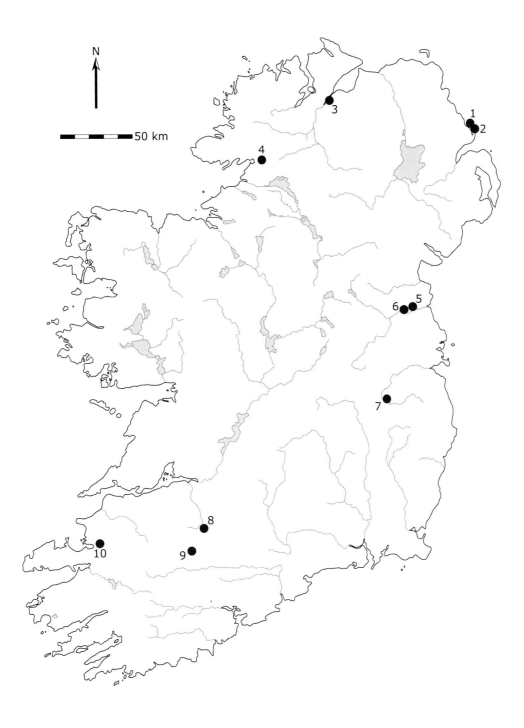

1 Island Magee, Co. Antrim; 2 Ballyharry, Co. Antrim; 3 Enagh, Co. Derry; 4 Drummenny Lower, Co. Donegal; 5 Townleyhall, Co. Louth; 6 Knowth, Co. Meath; 7 Corbally, Co. Kildare; 8 Tankardstown South, Co. Limerick; 9 Pepperhill, Co. Cork; 10 Cloghers, Co. Kerry.

Illus. 3—Map of Ireland displaying 10 Neolithic sites mentioned by Jones & Rowley-Conwy (2007, 396) from which cereal remains were recovered (the authors).

As part of the project, a comprehensive database is being established, recording the published and unpublished evidence for plant macro-remains in Neolithic Ireland (including cereal grains and chaff, nuts and nutshell, and weed and fruit seeds). Extensive radiocarbon dating of cereal remains is planned in order to establish the chronology of crop introduction and the spread of agriculture over the island. In terms of ancient farming practices, we will attempt to identify manuring and other management strategies. Manuring enriches the ratio of the heavier to the lighter stable isotope of nitrogen ($\delta^{15}N$) in the soil, which is then taken up by crops and can be detected through the analysis of surviving cereal remains (Bogaard et al. 2007). This is an innovative approach—representing the first time that such a study will be carried out on Irish material of any date—and will also contribute towards a wider European project examining this issue (entitled *Crop stable isotope ratios: new approaches to palaeodietary and agricultural reconstruction* and led by Bogaard). Analysis of arable weeds found alongside the cereal grains will also provide complementary insights into the nature, appearance, sowing regimes and longevity of ancient fields.

Furthermore, the project aims to collate published mammal bone evidence, as well as dietary evidence from human bone analyses, primarily stable isotopes but also dental pathologies such as caries rates, which relate in part to the consumption of carbohydrates. A re-evaluation of the Irish palaeoecological record—especially pollen studies and dendrochronological evidence—is in the process of being undertaken to examine the environmental (including climatic), chronological and landscape context of Neolithic farming. Available Neolithic and later radiocarbon dates in Ireland have been collated and analysed to explore the timing and intensity of activities throughout this period (Barratt et al., in prep.). Finally, we aim to re-examine available archaeological evidence relating to settlement and landscapes in the context of the above analyses. An important aspect of the project is the integration of environmental and archaeological evidence, which we anticipate will provide clearer insights into ancient farming practices, the environmental context of farming and the structuring of activities during the Neolithic period.

A wide range of analyses and approaches are being employed in this project, which requires expertise from many different areas of archaeological and related practice. We have therefore established a large project team to tackle these issues, consisting of researchers from a range of different sectors in archaeology and palaeoecology (including the state sector, an archaeological consultancy, and a range of Irish and British institutions).

Initial results from the newly established project

Since the project commenced, we have been collating evidence for cereal and other plant macro-remains from published and unpublished Neolithic archaeological excavations throughout Ireland. It has now been established that cereal remains have been recorded from a total of 41 sites of this period (Illus. 4), and this figure is likely to increase as work continues in tracking down unpublished data. It was previously noted that the most recent publication on this topic (Jones & Rowley-Conwy 2007) recorded cereal remains from only 10 Neolithic sites in Ireland; the new figure of 41 sites underlines the apparent widespread use of cereals in the past. A substantial number of these archaeological sites have been excavated in association with infrastructural projects carried out under the auspices of the NRA. As well as greatly increasing the number of known Neolithic houses and other

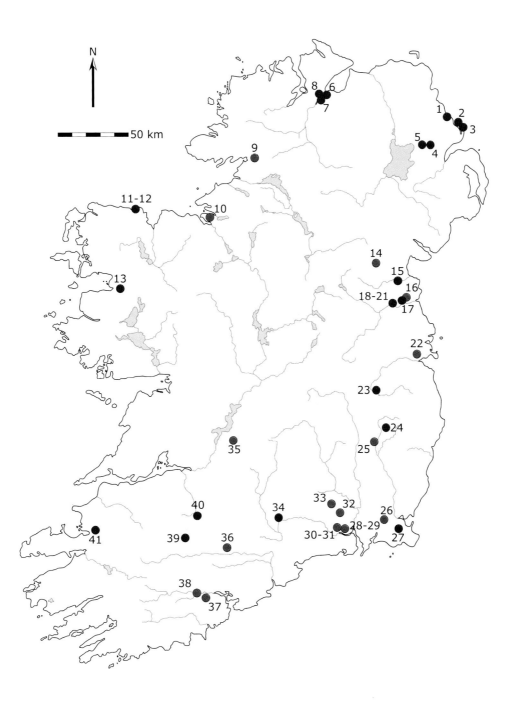

1 Ballygalley, Co. Antrim; 2 Island Magee, Co. Antrim; 3 Ballyharry, Co. Antrim; 4 Lyles Hill, Co. Antrim; 5 Donegore Hill, Co. Antrim; 6 Gransha, Co. Derry; 7 Enagh, Co. Derry; 8 Thornhill, Co. Derry; 9 Drummenny Lower, Co. Donegal; 10 Magheraboy, Co. Sligo; 11-12 (multi-phase) Ballyglass, Co. Mayo; 13 Gortaroe, Co. Mayo; 14 Monanny, Co. Monaghan; 15 Richardstown, Co. Louth; 16 Balgatheran, Co. Louth; 17 Townleyhall, Co. Louth; 18-21 (multi-phase) Knowth, Co. Meath; 22 Kilshane, Co. Dublin; 23 Corbally, Co. Kildare; 24 Baltinglass Hill, Co. Wicklow; 25 Russellstown, Co. Carlow; 26 Harristown Big, Co. Wexford; 27 Kerloge, Co. Wexford; 28-29 Newrath, Co. Kilkenny; 30-31 Granny, Co. Kilkenny; 32 Earlsrath, Co. Kilkenny; 33 Kilkeasy Co. Kilkenny; 34 Marlfield, Co. Tipperary; 35 Tullahedy, Co. Tipperary; 36 Gortore, Co. Cork; 37 Ballinaspig More, Co. Cork; 38 Barnagore, Co. Cork; 39 Pepperhill, Co. Cork; 40 Tankardstown South, Co. Limerick; 41 Cloghers, Co. Kerry.

Illus. 4—Map of Ireland displaying 41 Neolithic sites from which cereal remains were recovered. Sites excavated under the auspices of the NRA are marked in red (the authors).

settlement evidence, these NRA excavations have also uncovered more unusual sites, such as a causewayed enclosure at Magheraboy, Co. Sligo (MacDonagh 2005, 17–20; Danaher 2007, 89–127), and a possible causewayed enclosure at Kilshane, Co. Dublin, interpreted as a henge by the excavator (FitzGerald 2006, 33–5; Danaher 2007, 121). Analysis of remains from such a wide range of site types will enable an improved understanding of how cereals were used in a variety of circumstances. Work is ongoing and initial results from this and other aspects of the project are being prepared for publication (Whitehouse et al., in prep.).

Acknowledgements

Part of the research presented in this paper was funded by the Heritage Council under the INSTAR 2008 Programme (Ref.: 16682), awarded to Whitehouse, Schulting, Bogaard and McClatchie. Colleagues from the following organisations enabled access to unpublished data: NRA Archaeology Section; Archaeological Consultancy Services Ltd; Cultural Resource Development Services Ltd; Department of Archaeology, University College Cork; Eachtra Archaeological Projects; Headland Archaeology Ltd; Irish Archaeological Consultancy Ltd; Margaret Gowen & Co. Ltd; Northern Archaeological Consultancy Ltd; School of Archaeology, University College Dublin; and Valerie J Keeley Ltd. Additional input was provided by Project Partners in the *Cultivating Societies* project team: Sue Colledge (University College London); Dáire O'Rourke and Rónán Swan (NRA); Finola O'Carroll (Cultural Resource Development Services Ltd); Graeme Warren and John Ó Néill (University College Dublin); Paula Reimer, Finbar McCormick and David Brown (Queen's University, Belfast); Rob Marchant (University of York); and Alison Sheridan (National Museums Scotland). The cereal remains from Kerloge (Illus. 1) were excavated by Stafford McLoughlin Archaeology.

2. Early medieval food-processing technology at Kilbegly, Co. Roscommon: the miller's tale

Neil Jackman

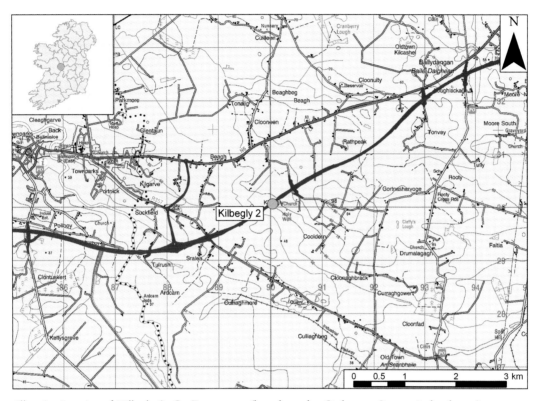

Illus. 1—Location of Kilbegly 2, Co. Roscommon (based on the Ordnance Survey Ireland map).

During archaeological testing in advance of the N6 Ballinasloe–Athlone road scheme in April 2007, structural timbers were revealed in a wetland area at the base of a hill in Kilbegly townland, Co. Roscommon, approximately 4 km east of Ballinasloe, Co. Galway (Illus. 1). These timbers were all extremely well preserved in shallow peat deposits. Fortuitously, they lay in a portion of a field used for pasture that had not been subject to significant agricultural works and had been largely unaffected by modern field drains on either side of them. Assessment of the timbers at the time of discovery indicated that they were the remains of a watermill. A full excavation was carried out by the author in conjunction with Caitríona Moore (archaeological woodworking consultant) on behalf of Valerie J Keeley Ltd for Galway County Council, Roscommon County Council and the NRA.[1] This excavation took place between May and September 2007 and a comprehensive post-excavation programme is currently under way. This paper serves as an initial discussion of what we found and highlights what this remarkably well-preserved site may tell us about some of the techniques and technologies used in early medieval milling in Ireland.

The excavation revealed the remains of a previously unknown early medieval horizontal mill (designated as Kilbegly 2), with its wheel-pit (or undercroft), flume (the

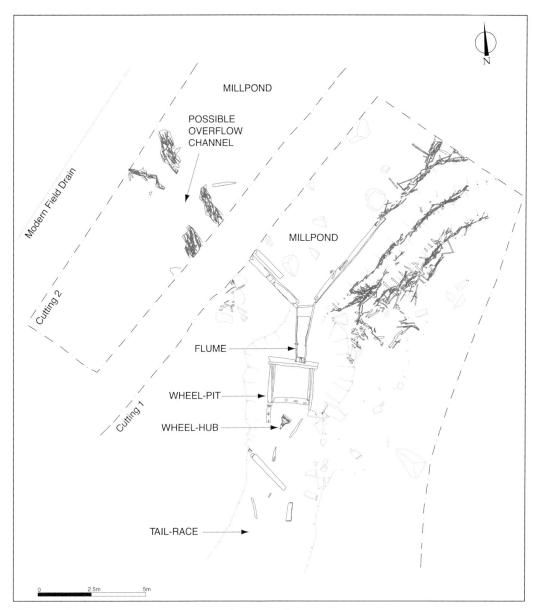

Illus. 2—Plan of the site during excavation (Valerie J Keeley Ltd).

wooden chute that carries the water into the wheel-pit), millpond, tail-race and other features preserved in their original locations (Illus. 2 & 3). A horizontal mill is a type of water-powered mill in which the wheel turned by the water rotates on a horizontal axis.

The sides of the millpond were lined with post-and-wattle and large oak timbers, each measuring 5 m long, which may have been salvaged by the millwrights from another early medieval building. The millpond had an estimated area of 340 m², but both its northern and eastern sides had been truncated and destroyed by early modern agricultural drains. A possible post-and-wattle overflow channel was identified running from the millpond, bypassing the wheel-pit and discharging into the tail-race. An overflow channel would have been essential as it allowed any water overflowing the millpond to be safely carried to the tail-race without damaging the mill building; it also enabled the millpond to be drained so that any necessary maintenance work could be carried out on the wheel-pit or flume.

Illus. 3—Archaeologists excavating and recording the horizontal mill at Kilbegly (Valerie J Keeley Ltd).

Two other post-and-wattle channels were identified to the east of the millpond. These had a north-east–south-west alignment and were approximately 8 m long and 1.2 m wide, with a varying depth of 0.45–0.65 m. They were constructed from varying-sized posts with up to 10 wattle rods woven around them. There was also evidence for the use of moss as a caulking agent on the interior of the channels, and compacted soil was piled around them to make them more watertight. These channels did not appear to be aligned with either the flume or the mill building, and at one point they connect to form a V-shape, so they are unlikely to have been mill-races. They may have served as a flood barrier, catching excess water before it damaged the mill building.

The millpond fed directly into the wooden flume, which was found in an excellent state of preservation (Illus. 4). It was a large piece of oak carved into a rectilinear box shape that narrowed towards the end. It had a separate lid secured in place by six wooden pegs. The flume measured 2.75 m in length and was wider at the end (0.65 m) where the millpond fed directly into it, narrowing at the end within the wheel-pit (0.45 m). It had an even height of 0.55 m and sloped at a 20° angle from the millpond to the wheel-pit. The end of the flume within the wheel-pit had a wooden plated aperture secured by iron rivets. The aperture had a subcircular opening with an approximate diameter of 0.2 m. The aperture plate was carved out of yew wood; as yew is a significantly harder wood than oak, it would have been more resistant to erosion. The aperture would have served primarily as a method of both directing and increasing the power of the flow of water onto the wheel-hub within the wheel-pit, in addition to the jet-deflector. The jet-deflector was a wooden wedge above the flume aperture that branched into two elements. Perforations were clearly evident on both of these and it is possible that a wooden bar suspending a flap ran through the

Illus. 4—The complete wooden flume (Valerie J Keeley Ltd).

Illus. 5—Remains of the wheel-pit, with the plated flume aperture at the back and the jet-deflector above it (Valerie J Keeley Ltd).

Illus. 6—The baseplates of the wheel-pit and flume following removal of the upper timbers (Valerie J Keeley Ltd).

perforations immediately in front of the flume's aperture. This would have been operated by a lever or rope so that the miller could start, adjust or cut off the water flow.

The wheel-pit was the lower floor of the mill building. Typically, the structure of an early medieval horizontal mill was separated into two floors; the upper floor is known as the mill-house, which contained the millstones and the grain hopper. Kilbegly, like every other early medieval horizontal mill excavated in Ireland, had no *in situ* remains of this floor; a possible wall or roof brace (also known as a cruck) was, however, recovered within the tail-race near to the building and may provide an indication of the building design of the mill-house. The wheel-pit housed the waterwheel, which was connected to the millstones in the upper floor by means of a wooden shaft. At Kilbegly the wheel-pit was extremely well preserved (Illus. 5), having three upstanding walls existing to a height of over 1 m. The walls were plank-built and set within large grooved baseplates (foundation timbers) (Illus. 6). The southern side of the wheel-pit appeared to have been left open; this would have facilitated the flow of water into the tail-race. The walls were directly above six floorboards of ash, which were

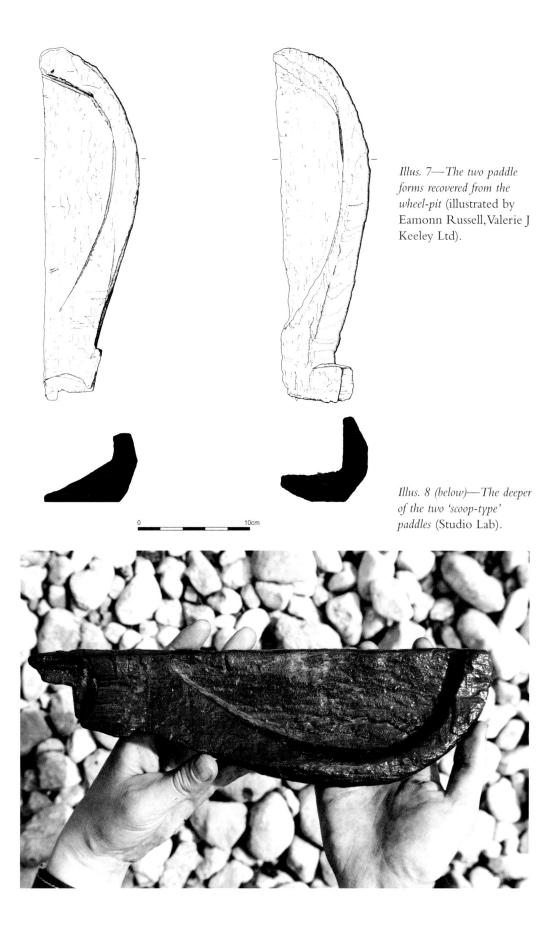

Illus. 7—The two paddle forms recovered from the wheel-pit (illustrated by Eamonn Russell, Valerie J Keeley Ltd).

0   10cm

Illus. 8 (below)—The deeper of the two 'scoop-type' paddles (Studio Lab).

particularly poorly preserved, in marked contrast to the more robust oak timbers recovered from the site. Two wooden wheel-paddles and a bell-shaped wheel-hub were retrieved from within the wheel-pit area, as were various wooden pegs and wedges and a possible stone gaming piece. The paddles and wheel-hub, in particular, are significant discoveries.

The paddles (Illus. 7) are of the 'scoop-type', and one is distinctly shallower than the other. It is possible that the deeper scooped paddle (Illus. 8) may have maximised the kinetic energy from a low water flow, whereas it would have been subject to far more pressure from a high water flow. In the latter case a shallow paddle would have been more efficient, creating less stress and wear on the paddle end and wheel-hub. This variance in paddle forms raises the question of technological choices. Were the paddles from different wheels? Were they constructed by different craftsmen, or were they fitted to the mill-wheel in response to two different water flows?

The hub of the mill-wheel is an outstanding example of early medieval woodworking technology (Illus. 9). It was carved from a block of oak into a bell shape that would have been far more hydrodynamically efficient than a simple disc. A total of 24 slots indicate that the hub may have held a maximum of 24 paddles. While cleaning the hub, however, it was discovered that only every second slot contained a wooden wedge. As no complete paddles were recovered in the hub, it is unknown whether the wedges would have served as supports or braces for the paddles. The paddles could have been interchangeable within the one hub depending on the water flow, with paddles added or removed as the circumstances dictated. Alternatively, they may have come from different hubs used at different phases during the mill's operational life.

Illus. 9—The wheel-hub discovered to the south of the wheel-pit (John Sunderland).

Once the water had passed through the wheel-pit it drained into the tail-race. This was a large, ditch-like feature cut into the natural subsoil. Within the excavation area the tail-race extended for 25 m but continued beyond the road corridor. It was 3 m wide and had a maximum depth of 1.5 m and ran roughly north-east–south-west. A wooden platform was identified within the tail-race approximately 5 m south-west of the wheel-pit. This was comprised of seven planks, with the largest seemingly bracing the other six. This feature may have served as an anti-erosion device, as it was situated next to a distinct downward fall within the tail-race, or it could possibly have been a fording point. A number of roughly dressed wooden poles discovered lying directly on top of

Illus. 10—Well-preserved wooden spade (John Sunderland).

the platform may have been the collapsed remains of a hand ropeway or other safety device. A fording point would have been necessary as the millpond, a working wheel-pit and the tail-race would have been significant obstacles to traverse.

A number of other clearly early medieval artefacts were recovered from the site, and not only inform our understanding of early medieval mill technology but also give a clear insight into diet, daily lives, agricultural implements and dress in the period. Finds include a copper-alloy ring-pin, withy ropes, fragments of leather (possibly from a bag or shoe), a whetstone, a wooden spade (Illus. 10), the previously mentioned gaming piece and bracelet fragments made from locally sourced shale.

The mill was situated in a wetland area at the base of a large hill. On the summit of the hill, approximately 600 m ENE of the mill, are the remains of an early medieval churchyard (Record of Monuments and Places Nos RO054-027001, -027002 & -027003). Another newly discovered site (Kilbegly 1), also excavated by the author, was identified on the slope of the hill, approximately 300 m north-east of the mill site.[2] This consisted of a number of small burnt pits and the shallow remains of an early medieval cereal-drying kiln. A kiln would have been an important part of the milling process, being used to dry the grain prior to grinding. Kilbegly 1 and the church may well be associated with the mill remains and may be indicative of the wider working landscape and agricultural practices of an ecclesiastical site.

The topographical positioning of the mill at Kilbegly indicates that the millwrights had a high level of surveying skill (for local site topography see Illus. 11). The site was not located on or by a river; instead, the millpond appears to have been fed by natural springs and the high water-table of the area. This is not the first early medieval horizontal mill in Ireland to be identified as non-riverine or non-tidal. Sites at Ballykilleen, Co. Offaly, and Ballygarriff and Coolnaha, Co. Mayo (C Rynne, pers. comm.), were also discovered to have been fed by natural springs and groundwater, and this certainly opens the possibility of more mills being discovered in marginal wetland areas near large secular or ecclesiastical sites.

The remains of up to nine early medieval watermills (vertical and horizontal) have been excavated recently on national road schemes (Murphy & Rathbone 2006; Seaver 2006) but the mill at Kilbegly 2 is the most outstanding example yet identified. The soil conditions, water-table and low-impact agricultural practices in the area since the site was abandoned

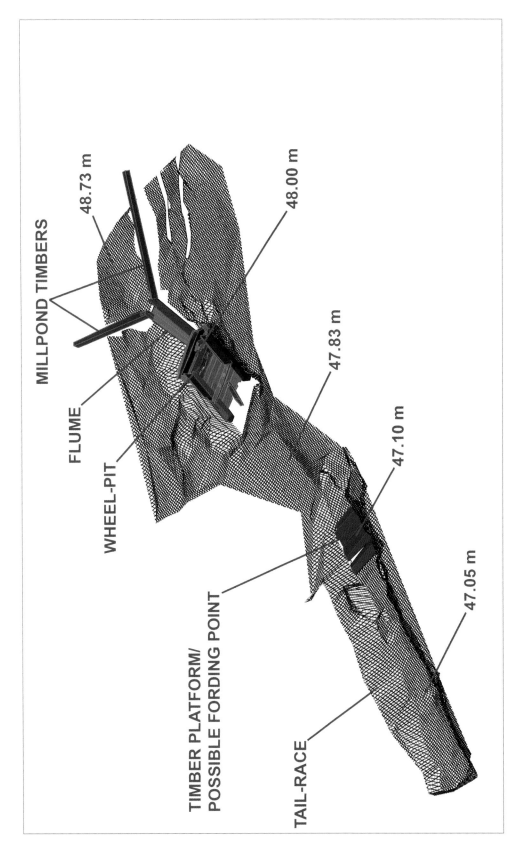

Illus. 11—A 3D representation of the local site topography at Kilbegly 2 (Valerie J Keeley Ltd).

meant that otherwise fragile structural elements and artefacts were excellently preserved and still in their near-original locations. Not only does the site inform us about early medieval milling technology, it also gives a wealth of information on carpentry techniques, being one of the best-preserved assemblages of worked wood from the period discovered in Ireland. Further analysis of this site should help to answer many questions about the techniques and technologies of early medieval milling, and the practice of cereal-processing generally. The excellent preservation conditions allow a range of palaeoenvironmental analysis and the results of this will be included in detail in forthcoming publications. Kilbegly 2 will be the subject of a full publication in due course, and all of the structural mill timbers and artefacts are currently undergoing a conservation programme with the aim of having a full reconstruction of the site on public display in the near future.

Acknowledgements

I would like to thank Galway County Council and Roscommon County Council, Martin Jones and Jerry O'Sullivan of the NRA and the engineering consultants Jacobs Engineering. Thanks are also due to the staff of the National Museum of Ireland, in particular Mary Cahill and Anthony Read for their advice and support throughout the excavation. I am extremely grateful to the specialists involved in the excavation project, including Caitríona Moore (woodworking), Ellen OCarroll (wood species analysis), Professor Michael O'Connell and Annette Overland (Palaeobotanical Department, NUI Galway), Susan Lyons (environmental analysis), Eileen Reilly (insect remains), John Sunderland (photography), Eamonn Russell (illustration), John Nicholl (leather analysis) and Stephen Mandal (stone artefacts). I am also indebted to Dr Colin Rynne (Department of Archaeology, University College Cork) for his assistance, knowledge and enthusiasm both during and after the excavation. I also wish to thank Senior Project Archaeologist Britta Schnittger, Site Surveyors Patrick Logue and Ronan Considine, and Graeme Laidlaw and Paul Stevens for commenting on an earlier draft of this text (all of Valerie J Keeley Ltd). Finally, many thanks must go to the excavation crew, in particular the Site Supervisors Roisin Burke and Connie Lubke.

Notes

1. Kilbegly 2: NGR 190038, 230053; height 49 m OD; excavation reg. no. E3369; ministerial direction no. A034.
2. Kilbegly 1: NGR 190147, 230150; height 57–62 m OD; excavation reg. no. E3329; ministerial direction no. A034.

3. Food for thought: newly discovered cereal-drying kilns from the south-west midlands

Patricia Long

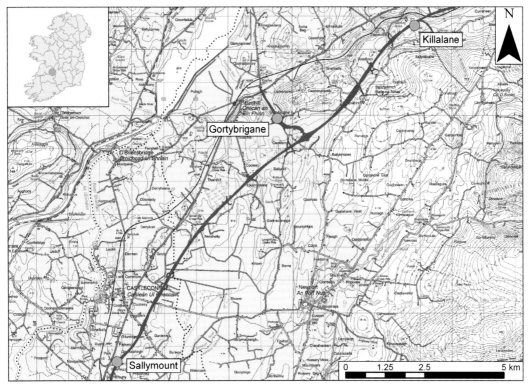

Illus. 1—Location of the sites at Gortybrigane and Killalane, Co. Tipperary, and Sallymount, Co. Limerick (based on the Ordnance Survey Ireland map).

Until recently the number of cereal-drying kilns known in Munster and Leinster was relatively low compared to the numbers known in northern Connacht and western Ulster (e.g. Johnston 2003; Monk & Kelleher 2005), but recent discoveries in advance of large infrastructural projects appear to have redressed this balance. It now seems that cereal-drying kilns were a common agricultural feature throughout the country, and the discovery of at least 21 such kilns along the route of the N7 Nenagh–Limerick High Quality Dual Carriageway is clear evidence that the south-west midlands were no exception. This paper will focus on seven of these kilns from four individual excavations directed by the author in the townlands of Sallymount, Co. Limerick, and Killalane and Gortybrigane, Co. Tipperary (Illus. 1). These excavations were conducted by Headland Archaeology Ltd on behalf of Limerick County Council in conjunction with North Tipperary County Council and the NRA. Although post-excavation analysis is still at a preliminary stage, the discovery of a variety of kiln types in a localised area has provided a valuable opportunity to examine the characteristics of cereal-drying kilns in this part of the country.

Cereal-drying kilns are generally classified according to their shape in plan (Monk & Kelleher 2005, 79). The categories of kiln are keyhole-shaped, L-shaped, figure-of-eight-shaped, dumb-bell-shaped and irregular (ibid.). Though these kilns varied in size and shape, they all functioned by directing heat from a fire, via a channel (or flue), to a drying chamber that would have contained the cereal. The crop would have been raised off the ground, on a timber drying floor for example, to allow the heat to permeate up through it. Interestingly, among the seven kilns under discussion here three different types were represented. Details of these kilns are summarised in Table 1.

Owing to the damp climate in Ireland cereal-drying kilns would have been an essential element in crop-processing (Kelly 2000, 241). Kilns were used to dry and ripen the harvest in wet years. Drying the cereal also facilitated processing, as the crop became brittle and the chaff was more easily removed; dry, brittle grain is also more suitable for milling (van der Veen 1989, 308). Lowering the moisture content of the grain made it less vulnerable to mould and fungus and prepared it for storage over the winter months, and the heat involved in the drying process had the added benefit of fumigating the crop of pests. Cereal-drying kilns were also used to kill off the shoots of germinating grains in the malting process (Johnston 2003, 3).

Table 1—Summary of the seven kilns within the study group.

Site	Kiln type	Orientation	Dimensions	Plant remains identified during preliminary assessment	Calibrated radiocarbon dates (2 sigma)
Killalane ringfort	Figure-of-eight	E–W	2.45 m long, up to 1 m wide and 0.3 m deep	Hulled barley as well as small amounts of rye	AD 654–768 (UBA-9931)
Gortybrigane enclosure	Dumb-bell	NW–SE	2.5 m long, up to 1.32 m wide and bowl 0.3 m deep	Hulled barley	AD 408–536 (UBA-9937)
Gortybrigane enclosure	Dumb-bell	NW–SE	2.5 m long, up to 1 m wide and 0.32 deep (in bowl)	Hulled barley	AD 430–570 (UBA-9936)
Gortybrigane enclosure	Keyhole (unlined)	NE–SW	2.29 m long, up to 1.33 m wide and 0.46 m deep (in bowl)	Hulled barley and oat	AD 542–633 (UBA-9938)
Sallymount enclosure	Dumb-bell	N–S	3.64 m long, 0.9–1.24 m wide and 0.68 m deep	Oat, hulled barley and possibly some rye	AD 653–770 (UBA-9935)
Sallymount enclosure	Dumb-bell	E–W	2.62 m long, 0.64–0.98 m wide and 0.46 m and 0.56 m in depth	Oat, hulled barley and possibly some rye	AD 688–870 (UBA-9934)
Killalane isolated kiln	Keyhole (stone-lined)	NNE–SSW	4.4 m long (including 2.9-m-long flue), 2.5 m wide and 0.36 m deep (in bowl)	No grain identified in preliminary assessment	AD 1688–1954 (UBA-9928)

The sites

Six of the seven kilns under discussion were found in association with three substantial ditched enclosures. On these sites it seemed that cereal-drying was taking place in a designated area within the settlement, slightly removed from dwellings and other industrial processes such as metalworking. Initial analysis would suggest that all three enclosures are early medieval in date but each was very different in character.

Enclosure at Killalane, Co. Tipperary

A figure-of-eight-shaped kiln was identified between the ditches of a bivallate enclosure at Killalane, Co. Tipperary.[1] Only that portion of the enclosure within the road corridor was excavated (Illus. 2). The south-west-facing entrance was flanked by two large post-holes that probably supported a gate structure. Initial interpretation of the site is that it was a bivallate ringfort. Inside the enclosure, evidence for a building and a large pit of uncertain function was identified. A whetstone and part of a rotary quern were the only artefacts recovered during the excavation. The rotary quern provides evidence that milling of grain was also taking place on the site.

The only feature identified between the two ditches was the figure-of-eight-shaped kiln (Illus. 3). One side of the kiln was disturbed by a modern drain but the western side remained intact. It is generally accepted that identifiable cereal-drying kilns consist of three components: a firing area (or firespot), a flue and a bowl/drying chamber (Monk & Kelleher 2005). The modern disturbance, however, made it difficult to identify these

Illus. 2—Elevated view of the bivallate ringfort at Killalane, Co. Tipperary, looking north (AirShots Ltd).

Illus. 3—Figure-of-eight-shaped kiln at Killalane (shaded to indicate its extent), with the remains of a possible clay roof around the edge of the drying chamber. The kiln had been truncated by a modern drain (Headland Archaeology Ltd).

elements in this particular kiln. A ring of clay around the western edge of the kiln may represent the remains of a clay roof over the drying chamber. The location of the kiln would have been slightly removed from the activity inside the enclosure and it may have been cut into the outer bank, which would have afforded it shelter and protection. There is, however, no stratigraphic evidence to support this idea and further dating analysis of the outer ditch is necessary in order to confirm contemporaneity with the kiln.

Enclosure at Gortybrigane, Co. Tipperary

Three cereal-drying kilns were identified within a large enclosure at Gortybrigane, Co. Tipperary.[2] Only part of this enclosure was excavated but a geophysical survey of the area beyond the road corridor indicated that it was subcircular in shape (Illus. 4). An unusual entrance was located on the north-east side, which had been modified during the enclosure's period of use. The geophysical survey indicated a possible second entrance on the south-west side.

Although the site had suffered severely from plough damage in the recent past, a large number of features were identified within the enclosure, including two structures (Illus. 5).

Illus. 4—Aerial view of the enclosure at Gortybrigane, Co. Tipperary, looking north-east, with a greyscale image of the geophysical survey results from the adjacent field (Markus Casey/Target Geophysics Ltd).

A number of features associated with metalworking were found in the north–west quadrant of the enclosure, while the three kilns were located in the south–east quadrant. This arrangement might suggest that the industrial processes of metalworking and cereal-drying were carried out within separate designated areas.

Two kiln types were represented at Gortybrigane: dumb-bell- and keyhole-shaped. Two dumb-bell-shaped kilns were identified and consisted of a depression at either end linked by a flue. The larger, more rounded of the depressions have been interpreted as the drying chambers.

Within the keyhole-shaped kiln, the circular south-western part of the feature has been interpreted as the drying chamber. Seven stake-holes identified at the base of the chamber would have supported a drying platform or superstructure, which is known to have existed in many keyhole-shaped kilns (Knox 1907). A subrectangular extension to the circular chamber would have served as the flue, though it was less than 0.9 m long. The base of the chamber was heavily oxidised, suggesting that high-temperature burning had taken place within it. A fire in the drying chamber would not have been the result of the cereal-drying process. The short length of the flue could have been the cause of an accidental fire. Experiments have shown that a spark from the firespot could easily have reached the bowl if the flue was short (Monk & Kelleher 2005).

A rotary quern base and two rotary quern fragments recovered on this site indicate that the milling of cereal was also taking place here.

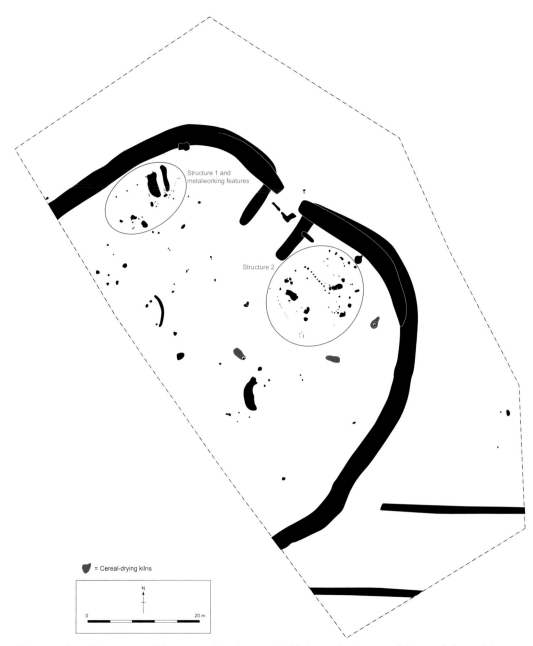

Illus. 5—Plan of the excavated features at Gortybrigane, highlighting the location of the cereal-drying kilns (Headland Archaeology Ltd).

Enclosure at Sallymount, Co. Limerick

Two dumb-bell-shaped kilns were identified within a structure in close proximity to a multi-phase enclosure site at Sallymount, Co. Limerick.[3] The main part of the enclosure was roughly circular in shape, with a small number of internal features, including a four-post structure of uncertain function. A subrectangular extension was added to the west of the enclosure and a number of features were also identified within this.

Three well-defined structures were located immediately south of the enclosure ditches (Illus. 6). The most westerly of these was rectangular with a central bowl furnace and large

Illus. 6—Aerial view of the enclosure at Sallymount, Co. Limerick, with structures and cereal-drying kilns highlighted (AirShots Ltd/Headland Archaeology Ltd).

amounts of metalworking waste deposited nearby. A regular nine-post structure was identified in the east of the site but there was no evidence as to the function of this building.

The third structure, located just outside the ditches of the subrectangular enclosure, seemed to have been designated for cereal-processing. Two kilns, positioned at a right angle to each other, were located at the east side of the building, which is likely to have been open-ended. A row of posts between the two kilns may represent a dividing wall within the structure. It is not yet clear whether this division served a particular function, such as the separation of grain types. The floor space within the structure to the west of the kilns could have been used for further processing, such as threshing or milling. Alternatively, it may have been used for grain storage, as has been suggested for structures associated with kilns at Rathbane South, Co. Limerick, and Haynestown, Co. Louth (Monk & Kelleher 2005, 84), even though this may only have been during seasons when the kilns were not in use owing to the risk of fire. Medieval texts indicate that grain was stored in a barn (*saball*) (Kelly 2000, 243), but clear evidence of such structures on archaeological sites is difficult to find. Light structures such as roof supports, screens or windbreaks have been identified on several sites (Monk & Kelleher 2005, 84), but the rectangular building surrounding the kilns at Sallymount was more substantial in nature. It is also possible that the nine-post structure to the east of the kilns and the four-post structure within the enclosure may have been grain stores, though there was no environmental evidence to support this. Similar four-post arrangements have been excavated elsewhere and interpreted as the foundations of grain silos (e.g. Gent 1983, 254).

Stone-lined kiln at Killalane, Co. Tipperary

The seventh kiln within the study group was found in relative isolation. It was a stone-lined, keyhole-shaped kiln that had been cut into a prehistoric burnt mound at Killalane.[4] It may have been sited here deliberately, as the mound would have appeared as a raised dry area in a generally wet field. It is possible that the kiln was related to a post-medieval farmstead that was excavated 200 m to the north, also in the townland of Killalane.[5]

A maximum of four courses of stone walling survived in the drying chamber, and the capstones on the flue had been displaced (Illus. 7). A rake-out deposit was located down-slope of the firespot, and this kiln also featured a stone baffle (barrier) that remained *in situ* between the flue and the drying chamber. The baffle would have prevented sparks from the fire from reaching the cereal in the chamber.

Illus. 7—Stone-lined cereal-drying kiln at Killalane during excavation (Headland Archaeology Ltd).

Dating and chronology

Monk and Kelleher (2005) have postulated that figure-of-eight- and dumb-bell-shaped kilns may have been the forerunners of keyhole-shaped kilns in Ireland. The seven kilns under discussion here have been radiocarbon-dated in an effort to contribute to the existing evidence of cereal-drying kiln chronology.

From the radiocarbon dates (Table 1) it seems that the earliest kilns within the study group were the two dumb-bell-shaped kilns in the Gortybrigane enclosure. Charred cereal grains from secure contexts within the kilns were dated, and these placed the kilns at the beginning of the early medieval period. Interestingly, the keyhole-shaped kiln within the same enclosure returned a slightly later date of AD 542–633 (UBA-9938; see Appendix 1 for details). The occurrence of two types of kiln within the same enclosure is significant and could be seen as direct evidence of kiln development. The figure-of-eight-shaped kiln at Killalane, however, post-dated the keyhole-shaped kiln at Gortybrigane, with a date of AD 654–768 (UBA-9931). The dumb-bell-shaped kilns in Sallymount, which were roughly contemporary with each other, had a similar date range.

The stone-lined, keyhole-shaped kiln at Killalane was considerably later than the other six kilns. It had a broad date range, though it is most likely to date from the 19th century. This date would generally be in keeping with other excavated keyhole-shaped kilns, which tend to date from the later and post-medieval periods (ibid., 105).

Although there is more post-excavation work to be done in relation to the dating of these kilns, the evidence so far would support the idea that the stone-lined keyhole-shaped kiln superseded figure-of-eight- and dumb-bell-shaped kilns. This is likely to have been a gradual process, and basic unlined keyhole-shaped kilns, such as that at Gortybrigane, may have been in use in parallel with older kiln types for a time, possibly indicating indigenous development of the keyhole-shaped kiln. The emergence of a preference for the keyhole-shaped kiln suggests that it was seen as the most efficient of the three types.

The plant remains

The preservation of plant remains on all four sites was poor, but preliminary assessment of charred grains by archaeobotanist Karen Stewart has given an indication of which crops were being processed in the kilns. Barley is the only crop so far identified from the early kilns at Gortybrigane. The later kiln on this site also had evidence for barley as well as oats.

The identifiable remains from the Sallymount kilns and the figure-of-eight-shaped kiln at Killalane were dominated by oats, with small amounts of barley. Evidence of rye and hazelnut shells was also present in very small amounts. In advance of charcoal identification, it is unclear whether the presence of hazelnuts was due to their use as a foodstuff or whether they were introduced through the use of hazel wood as fuel. It should be noted that a significant proportion of grains were unidentifiable during the assessment, but further analysis may provide more information. The plant remains from the stone-lined kiln at Killalane are currently undergoing analysis.

Overall, the evidence from these kilns suggests a dominance of barley in the three earliest kilns, while oat was dominant in the three slightly later kilns and there was no evidence of wheat.

Excavated cereal-drying kilns generally have a high incidence of oats, followed by barley and then wheat (Monk & Kelleher 2005, 85). Within the study group oats and barley also seem to have been prevalent in the kilns, although more analysis is required in order to comment further on the significance of the plant remains from these sites.

Conclusion

Cereal-drying kilns were a vital element in agricultural food production in Ireland's damp climate. Preliminary analysis of seven kilns on the route of the N7 Nenagh–Limerick road scheme has shown that the number and variety of kilns discovered in that area have the potential to contribute to our knowledge of kiln chronology and use on both a regional and national level.

Acknowledgements

I would like to thank the site supervisors and excavation crews involved in the sites discussed above, in particular Maura O'Malley, Barry Cosham and Lyndsey Clark. Thanks also to NRA Archaeologist Richard O'Brien and my colleagues at Headland Archaeology Ltd: Colm Moloney (senior archaeologist), Karen Stewart (archaeobotanist) and the graphics department. Finally, thanks to Jean Price and Damian Shiels for commenting on drafts of this paper.

Notes

1. Killalane enclosure: NGR 175839, 170715; height 73.47 m OD; excavation reg. no. E2495; ministerial direction no. A026.
2. Gortybrigane enclosure: NGR 171530, 167895; height 79.61 m OD; excavation reg. no. E2488; ministerial direction no. A026.
3. Sallymount enclosure: NGR 166520, 160525; height 38.95 m OD; excavation reg. no. E3420; ministerial direction no. A026.
4. Killalane kiln: NGR 175921, 170740; height 66.75 m OD; excavation reg. no. E2495; ministerial direction no. A026.
5. Killalane farmstead: NGR 175866, 170819; height 69.99 m OD; excavation reg. no. E2495; ministerial direction no. A026.

4. Geophysics, tillage and the ghost ridges of County Galway, c. 1700–1850

Jerry O'Sullivan

Illus. 1—Archaeologist Ronan Jones recording features observed in machine-cut test excavations at Rahally on the N6 Galway to Ballinasloe scheme (Galway County Council).

Geophysical survey and national road schemes

Intuition, experience and observation are among the ingredients in a successful field investigation. At the outset of a big development project, the field archaeologist uses all three in trying to predict what might be found on the development site. The sources of evidence include historic maps, aerial photographs, museum records, published local histories and anecdotal information from landowners. The archaeologist's own observations, from site inspections, are very important, but even the keen eyes of an experienced fieldworker cannot penetrate the soil. Ultimately, ground-breaking test excavations, by hand or machine (Illus. 1), are the most effective means of finding new archaeological sites, and such excavations are performed on the routes of all new national road schemes in advance of construction. (For more information on the archaeological assessment of road schemes see O'Sullivan 2007a.) There is one non-intrusive method, however, that has been described as 'seeing beneath the soil' (Clark 1990). This method employs geophysical survey equipment (Illus. 2) and has been widely used in Environmental Impact Assessments (EIAs) on road schemes in Galway and adjoining counties in recent years.

29

Illus. 2—Geophysical survey at archaeological reconnaissance stage on a national road project, using an FM256 Dual System Magnetometer (Earthsound Archaeological Geophysics, James Bonsall).

The geophysical survey methods deployed in our EIAs have included magnetic susceptibility, magnetic gradiometry and electrical resistivity, using a corresponding range of equipment in specialist hands. The common theme is that each of these methods measures some characteristic of the soil's natural electromagnetic field—or an induced field—in a search for anomalies that might have been caused by past events. These anomalies result from events that disturbed the ground or changed its characteristics. Buried hearths, wall foundations, boundary ditches or souterrains and other large voids can all be found by these means if conditions are favourable. Pyrotechnic features—like iron-smelting pits or pottery kilns—can give especially clear signals. Metal objects also give a very strong response, but these often turn out to be lost or discarded modern objects, ranging from old zinc buckets to an entire car that was buried in a field on the N6 Galway to Ballinasloe road scheme!

The specialists who performed or advised on these surveys for Galway County Council and the NRA did not agree about the best combination of methods or instruments to use. As a result, there was a degree of experimentation as our technique evolved from scheme to scheme. The schemes surveyed to date have a combined (centreline) length of 187 km and extend over an aggregate area of 1,856 ha. Taken all together, this is the basis for a fairly large experiment. In the end, we agreed that a centreline strip of recorded magnetic gradiometry, amounting to not less than 30% of the footprint of the road scheme (e.g. a continuous strip 15 m wide within a road corridor 50 m wide), was the optimum method at reconnaissance stage. Following the reconnaisance stage, on all schemes, we used magnetic gradiometry or electrical resistivity for detailed surveys in selected areas (Table 1). (We did not use ground-penetrating radar, although, with hindsight, this could have been very useful in some locations.)

So far, the results of this grand experiment have been variable and sometimes disappointing. Often, sites that were afterwards discovered by archaeological test excavations were not detected as geophysical anomalies at EIA stage. Conversely, many of the anomalies that were identified by geophysical survey proved to be non-archaeological in origin or could not be identified at all when tested afterwards by excavation. The largest of the surveys was also the most successful. On the N6 Galway to Ballinasloe scheme, areas amounting to 27.7% of the footprint of the scheme were surveyed using recorded magnetic gradiometry (Roseveare & Roseveare 2004a). The selected survey areas were chosen because there were known archaeological sites and monuments in the immediate vicinity, or historic population centres nearby, or simply because they lay within areas of good farmland that would also have been attractive to prehistoric and medieval settlers. Of the 202 geophysical anomalies that were detected by this survey, 63 were thought likely to be of archaeological origin, but as 14 of these were also known from other sources (e.g. map evidence or visible surface features) the number of anomalies of likely archaeological origin discovered exclusively by geophysical survey was 49. In the end, only eight (Table 2) of these turned out to be significant archaeological sites (i.e. sites where full archaeological excavation of a burial-ground, a settlement or industrial features took place).

Table 1—Geophysical survey methods on road schemes at Galway County Council NRDO.

Road scheme *Surveyors*	General reconnaissance	Targeted area surveys
N6 Loughrea Bypass *Roseveare & Roseveare 2003*	Magnetic susceptibility over 100% of the scheme	Magnetic gradiometry
N6 Galway to Ballinasloe *Roseveare & Roseveare 2004a*	Magnetic gradiometry over large areas amounting to 27.7% of the scheme	N/A
N6 Ballinsaloe to Athlone *Bonsall & Gimson 2004a*	Magnetic susceptibility centreline transects	Magnetic gradiometry
N6 Galway City Outer Bypass *Bonsall & Gimson 2006a*	Magnetic susceptibility centreline transects; magnetic gradiometry centreline ribbon	Magnetic susceptibility Magnetic gradiometry Electrical resistivity
N18 Oranmore to Gort *Krahn 2005*	Magnetic susceptibility centreline transects	Magnetic susceptibility Magnetic gradiometry
N18 Gort to Crusheen *Bartlett 2005*	Magnetic susceptibility Magnetic gradiometry	Magnetic gradiometry
N17 Tuam Bypass *Roseveare & Roseveare 2005b*	Magnetic susceptibility centreline transects; magnetic gradiometry centreline ribbon	Nil survey
M17 Galway to Tuam *Bonsall & Gimson 2006b*	Magnetic gradiometry	Magnetic gradiometry Electrical resistivity
N17 Castletown Realignment *Roseveare & Roseveare 2004b*	Magnetic gradiometry over 100% of the scheme	N/A
N84 Luimneagh realignment *Roseveare & Roseveare 2005a*	Magnetic susceptibility Magnetic gradiometry	Nil survey

Kevin Barton, Landscape & Geophysical Surveys, technical advisor to Galway County Council NRDO.

Table 2—Assessment methods and their results on the N6 Galway to Ballinasloe scheme.

Scheme details	
Area of road scheme	588 ha
Length of road scheme (centreline)	56 km
Number of fully excavated archaeological sites	37
Methods of discovery of significant excavation sites	
Test excavation	16
Desk study	8
Geophysical survey	8
Field inspection	4
Construction monitoring	1
Geophysical survey	
Combined areas of geophysical survey	163 ha (27.7%)
Criteria for selected survey areas	Good land
	Adjacent monuments
	Adjacent historic population centres
Survey method	Recorded magnetometry
Survey results	202 geophysical anomalies of all sorts
	63 possible archaeological sites
	49 sites identified by anomalies alone
	8 significant excavated sites = net result

Table 3—Archaeological geophysical survey results on road schemes at Galway NRDO.

Scheme	Potentially significant anomalies	Significant anomalies confirmed	Percentage anomalies confirmed
M17 Galway–Tuam (27 km)	77	Testing pending	n/a
N84 Luimneagh realignment (2 km)	9	Testing pending	n/a
N6 Galway City Outer Bypass (20 km)	22	Testing pending	n/a
N17 Castletown realignment (2 km)	4	0	0%
N17 Tuam Bypass (5 km)	12	0	0%
N6 Loughrea Bypass (5 km)	14	2	14%
N6 Galway–Ballinasloe (56 km)	63	8	13%
N6 Ballinasloe–Athlone (20 km)	10	1	10%
N18 Gort–Crusheen (22 km)	40	0	0%
N18 Oranmore–Gort (28 km)	19	0	0%
Totals	158	11	7%

Note—the figures in the 'Significant anomalies confirmed' column refer to archaeological sites discovered primarily by geophysical survey and do not include sites that appeared in geophysical survey results but that were also known from other sources of information.

Eight excavated archaeological sites may seem a poor return from 202 anomalies, but as only 30 other significant sites were excavated (i.e. sites discovered from desk-based sources, field inspection, test excavations or construction monitoring) these eight sites amounted to 21% of all of the archaeological sites discovered on the scheme. Arguably, the proportion would have been higher if all of the scheme had been surveyed and not merely the most promising 27.7% of its total area. On the other hand, it must be conceded that the results of surveys on other schemes have been much less impressive, with the number of significant archaeological sites discovered exclusively by geophysical survey being as low as two, or one, or none (Table 3). This is partly due to the methods used (it is acknowledged that magnetic susceptibility was a poor choice for the reconnaissance stage of the surveys) but also relates to ground conditions. Some of the lands traversed by these schemes include large tracts of peatland or peaty soils that have been reclaimed for pasture, especially on the N6 Ballinasloe to Athlone scheme in south Roscommon (Bonsall & Gimson 2004a). Elsewhere there are large tracts of improved pasture with thin soils overlying karstic limestone bedrock or unimproved boulder fields with expanses of protruding bedrock, especially on the N18 Oranmore to Gort and N18 Gort to Crusheen schemes (Krahn 2005; Bartlett 2005).

Was this grand experiment a success? Can we justify persisting with these extensive surveys on every new scheme? The answer is certainly yes, and for several reasons. Firstly, the surveys are not expensive. The value for money in any archaeological investigation is measured by its results. The cost of an extensive geophysical survey on a road scheme will typically be about 1.5% of the total archaeological costs, so that even a modest result can justify the outlay and, in at least one instance, on the N6 Galway to Ballinsaloe scheme (above), the results have been very good indeed. Secondly, any experimental results are reliable in proportion to the volume of data on which they are based. To break off a procedure midway in the process merely because one is disappointed by the results is poor science. Thirdly, it may be a mistake to think that geophysical anomalies do not correspond to archaeological features merely because they cannot afterwards be confirmed by test excavation. One thing that we discovered is that the soil is full of 'ghost' features that are only detectable as geophysical anomalies and by no other means. It would be rash to dismiss them from the record merely because their definition is not improved by probing with the bucket of a 20-tonne tracked excavator. Indeed, it can be argued that a survey method that identifies features not susceptible to any other means of detection is the most valuable of all assessment methods, because it hints at stories that would otherwise be overlooked. The 'ghost ridges' of this paper will illustrate the point.

Ghost ridges

A type of feature identified by all of the surveys is the distinctive corduroy striping of cultivation furrows (Illus. 3 & 4). These occur very widely in the study areas, on every hillside and valley bottom that was surveyed. This 'striping' of the landscape by tillage, in our geophysical survey plots, seems odd to contemporary eyes, because Galway and the adjoining counties are predominantly pastoral places today. Older country people remember a time, not more than 35 years ago, when farming in the West involved a mixed regime of cattle, sheep and pigs, with fruit, root and cereal crops being grown for the market, for the table or for exchange with neighbours. Since that time, changing agriculture policy, EC/EU grants and market demand have combined to transform the farming landscape of the West into a monoculture of improved grass pasture for livestock—predominantly dry cattle and some sheep. These days, a person could walk all day through the countryside in County Galway and not see a tilled field or a standing crop (Illus. 5).

So what are these tillage features seen everywhere in our surveys? When were they formed? Why are they found so extensively? And what sort of tillage regime do they represent? Physically, they can be defined as broad-ridge remnants, at intervals of c. 2–4 m, forming straight or parallel groups and extending over large areas. Sometimes they are found to respect the existing field boundaries (usually drystone field walls of 18th- or 19th-century date) and sometimes they pre-date them. Frequently they form a palimpsest of

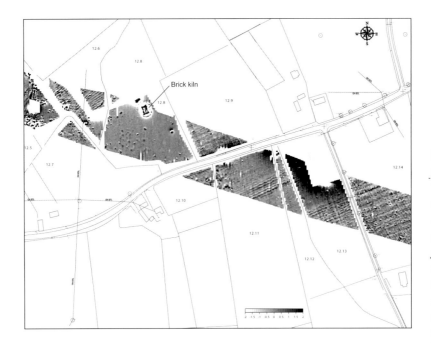

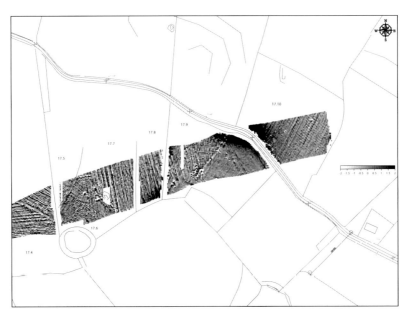

Illus. 3—Pyrotechnic features, like this Victorian brick kiln at Brusk (top), appear as strongly defined anomalies in geophysical survey results, but the corduroy striping of early modern cultivation ridges, like this example from Rahally (bottom), occurs very extensively in all of the surveys from Galway and adjoining counties. Both examples are from a survey of the N6 Galway to Ballinasloe scheme (Roseveare & Roseveare 2004a).

Illus. 4—Broad, mounded, spade-dug ridges can still be seen here and there in lands that have now reverted to pasture (above) or in marginal lands that have not been ploughed in the modern period (below) (Galway County Council).

Illus. 5—Pasture for drystock farming (above) has almost entirely replaced tillage in modern farming in the West, so that it is possible to walk all day across country in County Galway today (below) and not see a tilled field or standing crop (J O'Sullivan).

superimposed groups, where the ridges have evidently been laid out first in one direction and then in another in successive seasons. Remnant ridges are sometimes visible as surface features, but never to the extent revealed in the geophysical surveys. And very often the furrows cannot be detected as 'cut' features in the soil profile, even when they are exposed by machine-testing—hence their description as 'ghost ridges' in this paper, adopting an expression used by some geophysical surveyors in describing anomalies that are detectable but not visible (Schleifer 2004; Bonsall & Gimson 2004b). Possible causes of our ghost ridges are organic manures, which would have influenced the iron content of the soils, and ashes arising from sod or stubble burning, which would have increased the soil magnetic susceptibility of ashy silt deposits forming in furrow bottoms.

From their extent, form and relationships with extant field boundaries, it can be concluded that the ridges and furrows most frequently seen in our geophysical survey results are not ancient features but date broadly from the early modern period (c. 1700–1850), when there was a tremendous increase in the amount of arable farming in Ireland. Several authorities have written about the methods and equipment used in early modern Irish farming, including Evans (1957), Lucas (1970), Ó Danachair (1970), Gailey (1982) and Bell (Bell 1984; 2008; Bell & Watson 1986). What follows here, in the short space available, is necessarily a superficial treatment of a complex subject. Readers are strongly recommended to these authorities for a more detailed treatment, and to the early modern writers from whom today's scholars derive much of their information—like Arthur Young (1776–9), Hely Dutton (1824) and Horatio Townshend (1810); and also to *Feast and Famine*, an excellent book on the history of Irish food by L A Clarkson & E Margaret Crawford (2001).

Tillage in the West, c. 1700–1850

The most striking feature of the tillage regime represented in our surveys is that it was extremely labour-intensive. The population of Ireland grew from an estimated one million in 1650 to 8½ million in 1845. Labour was cheap and easily available. Arable land in the West was commonly worked not by ploughing with teams of draught animals but by hiring gangs of agricultural labourers—both men and women—who broke the ground with heavy, long-handled spades and mounded the soil into long, straight, broad ridges (Illus. 6). They sometimes worked collectively, going all together from farm to farm to hire themselves out as a team. Hely Dutton could report to the Royal Dublin Society in his *Statistical and Agricultural Survey of the County of Galway* (1824, 62–3): 'Some of the better kind of farmers use the plough for this purpose, but the general mode is by the spade or loy. When labourers work by the day, it may probably take from thirty to forty men per acre.'

The straight sets of ridges that typically result from spade-dug tillage are not to be confused with medieval broad ridges. Some very broad, curvilinear ridges are recorded in Ireland in the early modern period, but straight ridges were the norm by c. 1800 (Bell 1984, 23). In general, broad S-shaped ridges are the signature of lowland medieval estate farming, and these were permanent features, built up over the years by repeated traverses with a mould-board plough. Likewise, our ridges are not to be confused with 'lazy beds', a very particular kind of ridge that was formed by turning the sod upon itself to form the ridge, thus leaving a very wide furrow between each planting bed. This kind of ridge was used especially for potatoes—both in subsistence cultivation by the poorest folk and also, more

Illus. 6—Women at work in 1901 on cultivation ridges in Glenshesk, Co. Antrim (R J Welch Collection RW.1164, Ulster Museum).

extensively, to 'clean' the weeds from fallow land with a potato crop before subsequent seasons of cereal-planting. The differences between one kind of cultivation ridge and another are seldom clear-cut, however, and Bell (ibid., 21–2) is worth quoting at length in this regard:

> Techniques of making ridges varied widely throughout Ireland, as did their dimensions when complete. The latter applied even when the same crop was being cultivated. In 1774, for example, Hyndman discussed the cultivation of flax on ridges ranging from three feet to twenty-three feet in width. Very broad ridges were recorded in Kilkenny, where some 'gentlemen' farmers practised a technique of ploughing 'in balk' for corn crops. The ridges made were up to 16 yards wide. In the mid 19th-century, however, the agriculturalist Martin Doyle claimed the commonest Irish practice was to make 'extremely narrow' ridges, about four feet in width. Unfortunately, the width of trenches or furrows, separating ridges, was more rarely noted by observers. Arthur Young recorded ridges six feet wide, which were separated in one instance by furrows two feet in width, in another, two and a half feet. It seems to have been fairly common for narrower ridges to be accompanied by furrows which were between one third and one half the ridges' breadth. Ridges also varied in height. The rather fragmentary evidence suggests that the centres of ridges might be anything from six inches to three feet higher than the adjoining furrow bottoms.

This was a very aggressive regime in its treatment of the soil profile. The sets of ridges in a field were not permanent. From season to season their orientation might be changed or,

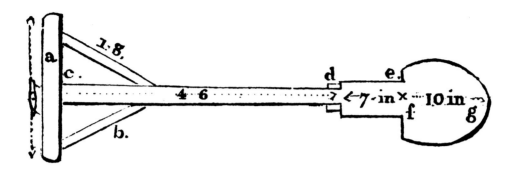

Illus. 7—A 'flatcher' from County Tyrone: this heavy instrument was in effect a breast plough, used to pare the sod from fallowed land in preparation for spade-dug cultivation ridges (reproduced from McEvoy 1802, 51).

after a fallow period, the sod might be pared off the surface then piled, dried, burned and spread again as fertiliser. The furrows between the ridges might be deepened to bring up mineral-rich subsoils, which were also spread on the ridges as fertiliser, and drains were sometimes set between the ridges in the deepened furrows. (As an aside, this aggressive treatment of the soils in the early modern period may partly explain why earth-cut features from earlier periods—like the post-pits of a prehistoric roundhouse, for instance—are so seldom found by test excavations in the West.)

Intensive manual tillage required a distinctive set of tools. The instrument for paring sod (a 'flatcher') was a kind of heavy, wooden breast-plough with a wide curved blade (Illus. 7). At harvest time sickles were preferred to scythes. A large scythe in experienced hands is five times more efficient than a sickle but is not convenient for use on rounded, steep-sided ridges. The local forges known as 'spade mills'—where agricultural tools were manufactured or finished—flourished in this period (Rynne 2006, 268; O'Sullivan et al., forthcoming). Spades themselves varied considerably in their design, not only from region to region but from one district to another, and different sorts of spade might be used in the same field for breaking the ground, ditching a furrow, raising a ridge and working the tilth on its surface. Sometimes the spade and plough were combined, as in this modern instance reported by Jonathan Bell (correspondence 29/10/2004): 'We have recorded one man in Monaghan who made one side of the ridge using a horse plough, going downhill, and the other side using a spade, and a lot of ridges were started by ploughing and finished by spades'.

Why was this seemingly archaic way of tilling the land preferred in the West? The answer is in the sky and in the soil. Then, as now, the West of Ireland can experience up to 60% more rainfall—and correspondingly less sunshine—than the driest parts of the South and East. Wet soil is cold, and the crops it supports are more prone to disease and failure. The 'Improvers' of the day—agricultural innovators and applied theorists—railed against what they perceived as archaic methods. Horatio Townshend, in his *Statistical Survey of the County of Cork* (1810, 247), complained that: 'An experienced agriculturalist cannot behold without surprise, a farmer with half a dozen labourers, toiling for a fortnight (while his horses are doing nothing), to perform a piece of work, which his plough and harrow could accomplish in a couple of days'. Yet it is a fact that soil in mounded ridges is warmer and drier than the same soil spread in a flat tilth. Also, ridges expose the crop to more light and air, which is an added benefit in a damp climate. A cost-benefit analysis by the Devon

Commission in 1847 determined that the labour used to make ridges could more profitably be diverted to drainage work instead, with the aim of making ridges redundant within a period of 20 years (quoted in Bell 1984, 27). But in the absence of public monies to bring about these improvements, the first concern of farmers was with immediate profit and not with the fortunes of the next generation. They understood, from experience, that they could recoup the high cost of making ridges from the bigger yield obtained at harvest time, and this was sometimes acknowledged by the 'improvers' too.

In general there was a big increase in the amount of land brought under cultivation in Ireland in this period and a corresponding increase in the volume of root and cereal crops produced. Partly the increase in tillage was led by market demand. Over 200 breweries and about 2,500 grain mills are recorded in Ireland by the mid-19th century (Rynne 2006, 241, 256), but Irish oats, barley and wheat were also being exported on a large scale to mills and breweries in Britain in this period. Tillage did not supplant livestock husbandry in western counties but they did participate in the general increase in arable production at this time. The crops grown in Galway were much as elsewhere in the country. Hely Dutton's *Survey* (1824, 12) recorded that: 'The soil of this county generally produces every crop in abundance. The wheat, particularly that which is produced to the southward of Galway, is amongst the best in Ireland, producing that fine bread to be found in Galway, Tuam and other towns, and in almost every gentleman's house.'

The increase in tillage was also led by subsistence needs. Spade-dug cultivation techniques were used on a large scale in the West, alike by tenant farmers on 10 acres and gentlemen farmers on landed estates. But as the population grew, more and more land came under cultivation, so that remnant ridges can still be seen today in the most unpromising locations, on steep-sided hills, dry knolls in bogs and cleared patches in boulder fields, where marginal land was broken and planted by the poorest folk, to grow food for themselves. Oats had been the staple of the ordinary Irish in the post-medieval period but gave way to potatoes as the early modern period advanced; buttermilk was their drink in both periods. The poor ate very little else. But subsistence and the market did not represent separate, unrelated economic worlds. They were interwoven by labour in a manner starkly described by Robert Bell in the 1790s:

> Bread made of flour of wheat was a luxury; but whenever, by any uncommon effort [the labourer] was able to cultivate that species of grain, it bore a price at market so comparatively high, that ruin would to him be the consequence of not selling the whole of it. Hardly ever in the possession of any sort of flesh meat, but pork or bacon, he always considered this as an article of too much value to be converted to the use of himself or his family. The butter, the poultry, and the eggs, were equally his property, and the miserable family by whose care they were produced, were equally prohibited to use them. What did these people live on? They lived on those things for which little or no money could be procured at market: potatoes constituted their chief food. The next article which he retained for his own use was one of still less value, it was that part of the milk which remained behind after butter had been extracted from it [quoted in Clarkson & Crawford 2001, 86; after Bell 1804].

Hely Dutton (1824, 70) complained that he had heard Galway's landlords too often say of their tenants: "I do not care a damn what they do, or how dirty their houses are so [long as] I receive my rents". By the eve of the Famine, 40% of Irish farms were less than 10 acres in extent and almost none were owner-occupied (Rynne 2006, 187). Cottars lived on much less. So long as potatoes were plentiful, labour was cheap and the land was tenanted, not owned, by the people who farmed it, the increases in demand for arable products did not spur on either innovations in technique or investments in improvements.

So what brought the archaic and labour-intensive regime of manual tillage to an end? A constellation of factors combined to make the gangs of hired labourers with their heavy, long-handled spades a thing of the past. Extensive drainage schemes were got under way in the West as the 19th century advanced, with corresponding improvements in the soils. In tandem with drainage schemes, roads and trackways were developed, so that farmlands became accessible to mechanised equipment and wheeled vehicles. Mechanical equipment, like steam-driven ploughs and harrows, became available to estates and larger farms, and on smaller holdings the light, iron, Scottish 'swing plough'—which could be operated efficiently by a ploughman with a single draught horse—was universally adopted. (This is the light, elegant iron plough most often seen today blocking gaps in hedgerows or discarded in farmyards, but still used by its aficionados in exhibitions at ploughing matches.) Scythes or reaping machines replaced the sickle. Market demands changed too, so that dairy and meat products increasingly displaced cereals in the Irish export market. (In the later 19th century Ireland became for the first time a net importer of cereals.) But critically, the great Famine of 1845–8 brought an end to the plentiful supply of cheap labour on which, above all, spade-dug tillage had depended.

Today, it is still possible to see fugitive patches of broad ridges in parts of County Galway—usually in marginal land that was brought into cultivation by the poorest people, at a time of peak population, but that has only been used since then for rough grazing. Elsewhere, the swathes of corduroy-striped cultivation ridges that once covered the land, and the people too who made them, have become ghosts in the landscape, and are only made visible again in the greyscale images of our geophysical survey reports.

Acknowledgements

The archaeological geophysical surveys commissioned on national road schemes by Galway County Council NRDO were performed by ArchaeoPhysica Ltd (supported by Substrata Ltd), Earthsound Archaeological Geophysics, Minerex Geophysics Ltd (supported by Moore Environmental & Archaeological Services Ltd and Eastern Atlas Geophysikalische Prospection), and the Bartlett–Clark Consultancy for RSK ENSR Environment Ltd. The technical adviser to the Council for these surveys was Kevin Barton of Landscape and Geophysical Surveys.

5. *Fulachta fiadh* and the beer experiment

Billy Quinn and Declan Moore

Illus. 1—A fulacht fiadh/*burnt mound excavated at Raheenagurren West, Co. Wexford, on the route of the N11 Gorey–Arklow Link Road* (Valerie J Keeley Ltd).

Fulachta fiadh, or burnt mounds, generally date from the Bronze Age and are one of the most widespread of Irish field monuments, perhaps numbering up to 5,000. Of the 500 or so sites currently entered in the NRA Archaeological Database (www.nra.ie/Archaeology/NRAArchaeologicalDatabase/, accessed August 2008), 28% are *fulachta fiadh* (with associated features) or burnt mounds/spreads (with no associated features). To date, they have been excavated on road schemes in 18 counties, in all provinces. Typically, a *fulacht fiadh* site is defined by a low, horseshoe-shaped mound. Upon excavation the mound is found to consist of charcoal-enriched soil and heat-shattered stone around a central trough (Illus. 1 & 2).

The name derives from Geoffrey Keating's 17th-century manuscript *Foras Feasa ar Éirinn* and as a complete term does not appear in any early manuscripts (Ó Néill 2004). Conventional wisdom, based largely on Professor M J O'Kelly's 1952 experiments in Ballyvourney, Co. Cork, suggests that they were used for cooking (ibid.; O'Kelly 1954). Alternative theories that have been proposed include bathing, dyeing, fulling and tanning. It is, however, generally agreed that their primary function was to heat water by depositing fired stones into a water-filled trough. In this paper we would like to explore a further hypothesis, reported previously elsewhere (Quinn & Moore 2007): were some *fulachta fiadh* prehistoric micro-breweries?

Illus. 2—Archaeologists excavating the trough of a fulacht fiadh/*burnt mound uncovered at Newrath, Co. Kilkenny, on the route of the N25 Waterford City Bypass* (James Eogan).

So where does beer come into it?

In order to answer this we have to look into the natural history and archaeology of intoxication. The inebriation of animals has been documented anecdotally (Dudley 2004) but has received little scientific attention. There is evidence from around the world of animals experiencing drunkenness as a result of consuming overripe fruit containing yeast (producing ethanol), resulting, unsurprisingly, in inebriation.

Indeed, what may have been drunken behaviour by howler monkeys in Panama's Barro Colorado Island was observed by Dustin Stephens, leading Stephens and Robert Dudley of the University of California, Berkeley, to the preliminary conclusion that preference for and excessive consumption of alcohol by modern humans might accordingly result from pre-existing sensory biases associating ethanol with nutritional reward (Stephens & Dudley 2004). Put simply, the so-called 'drunken monkey hypothesis' suggests that natural selection favoured primates with a heightened sense of smell for psychoactive ethanol, indicative of ripe fruit, who would thus have been more successful in obtaining nutritious fruit!

Early hunter-gatherers had an intimate knowledge of the environment around them and the effects of naturally occurring intoxicants, but the discovery of fermentation may simply have been a happy accident involving overripe fruit. As agriculture took root, however, barley and wheat became plentiful, which in turn provided good substrates for beer or ale.

There's no doubt that people were drinking beer throughout the world in prehistory. As Pete Brown says in *Man Walks into a Pub* (2003), 'even elephants eat fermenting berries deliberately to get p★★★★d and we are much more cleverer than them [sic]'.

Recent chemical analyses of residues in pottery jars from a Neolithic village in northern China revealed evidence of a mixed fermented beverage from as early as 9,000 years ago (McGovern et al. 2004). Clear chemical evidence for brewing in Sumeria at Godin Tepe (in modern-day Iran) comes from fermentation vessels where there were pits in the ground noted by the excavators (Michel et al. 1992). In the *Hymn to Ninkasi* (Civil 1964) by a Sumerian poet (dated to 1800 BC) and found written on a clay tablet is one of the most ancient recipes for brewing beer using pits in the ground:

'You are the one who handles the dough,
[and] with a big shovel,
Mixing in a pit, the bappir with sweet aromatics'.

In north-western Europe there is evidence of Neolithic brewing at Balbirnie in Scotland and at Machrie Moor, Arran, where organic residue impregnated in sherds of Grooved Ware pottery were described as 'perhaps the residues of either mead or ale' (Hornsey 2003, 194). Based on the highly decorated, beaker-shaped pottery vessels characteristic of the Bronze Age Beaker Culture, it has even been suggested that Beaker people traded in some sort of alcoholic beverage and that the beakers may have been high-status drinking vessels.

Regarding Ireland, the first known reference to beer is in AD 1 (Griffiths 2007, 11), when Dioscorides (a Greek medical writer) refers to 'kourmi' (a plain beer, probably made from barley), although Nelson (2005, 51, 64) relates this as a reference to Britain. Much later, St Patrick appears with 'the priest Mescan . . . his friend and his brewer'. Perhaps unsurprisingly, Patrick considers his friend and brewer to be 'without evil' (www.mohurley.blogspot.com/2009/03/from-annals-of-4-masters-st-patrick.html, accessed April 2007).

As Zythophile points out in his post 'St. Brigid and the Bathwater' in the blog 'Zythophile' (http://zythophile.wordpress.com/2008/01/22/st-brigid-and-the-bathwater/, accessed March 2008), ale was an important part of Irish society. He notes that the *Crith Gablach* (a seventh-century legal poem), for example, declared that the 'seven occupations in the law of a king' were:

'Sunday, at ale drinking, for he is not a lawful flaith [lord] who does not distribute ale every Sunday; Monday, at legislation, for the government of the tribe; Tuesday, at fidchell [a popular early medieval board game]; Wednesday, seeing greyhounds coursing; Thursday, at the pleasures of love; Friday, at horse-racing; Saturday, at judgment.'

Sundays and Tuesdays must have been particularly taxing.

The following jumped out and we were surprised we hadn't noticed it:

'A record of a fire at the monastery of Clonard . . . around AD 787 speaks of grain stored in ballenio, literally "in a bath", which seems to mean the grain being soaked as part of the initial processes of malting'.

Zythophile suggests that what St Brigid drew off may have been water from the ballenium where the grain was steeping in the first stage of malt-making.

The great mystery of prehistoric brewing

In prehistoric times until the late Iron Age, metallurgy was limited to small hand tools and high-status items. Throughout prehistoric Europe one of the main challenges for the brewer (in the absence of suitable metal containers) was the heating of large volumes of water to make a wort (see below). Indeed, given that brewing until the modern era was a home-based industry, sufficiently large metal mash tuns (watertight containers) were uneconomical. So how could people brew without the application of direct heat? Hot rocks are the most logical means.

A simple web search gave us some quick answers. Today the only commercial hot-rock brewery in the world (as far as we know) is Boscos Brewery in Nashville. Here the master brewer uses Colorado Pink Granite to heat the mash. The stones are heated in a brick oven and added to the mash (see below) in a process known as decoction, whereby the temperature is gradually raised over a period of time. Further evidence of hot-rock brewing comes from Finland, where *Sahti*, a vernacular, unhopped ale, is still served at rural feasts (www.brewingtechniques.com/library/styles/6_4style.html, accessed April 2007). Again the ale is prepared by immersing hot rocks into a wooden mash tun; the resulting wort is then flavoured by filtering it through juniper branches. The brewing of *Sahti* has been traced back over 500 years. Although *Sahti* is specifically linked to Finland, ales using similar brewing methods were brewed throughout the Baltic States and as far south as Ossetia in modern Georgia.

With so many comparative ancient and contemporary processes involving pits in the ground or wooden troughs and hot-rock brewing technology, we reached the not-unreasonable conclusion that *fulachta fiadh* would make ideal micro-breweries.

So how do you brew a prehistoric beer?

Beer at its simplest requires the following ingredients: milled, malted grain (preferably barley but wheat will do), copious amounts of reasonably clean water, yeast to aid fermentation and herbal flavouring. The latter ingredient is not an essential component in brewing but bitter-tasting dried leaves were traditionally added to counter the sweetness of the brew and increase palatability. At the processing stage the conditions and equipment required are a preparation area for malting (an aired, indoor floor space where the saturated grain can be dried and lightly roasted), firewood for heating stones, a large, watertight wooden container or mash tun, a paddle for stirring and some earthenware fermentation vessels (Illus. 3).

The fundamentals of brewing necessitate converting the starch in the malted grains into soluble sugars. This is achieved by adding the milled, malted grain to a container of hot water heated to a temperature of approximately 67°C. This mix is then mashed or agitated with a paddle, producing a glucose-rich syrupy solution known as a wort. The wort is then transferred into storage vessels, where the yeast and flavourings are added, and allowed to stand for several days, during which fermentation will naturally occur. During this stage the brew begins to fizz and froth as the active yeast devours the sugars and excretes alcohol. When the fizzing subsides, the fermentation is complete and the end product is unhopped ale.

Hot-rock technology has been used by primitive communities throughout the world and involves heating fist-sized stones in a fire, removing them with a tongs or a fork and

Illus. 3—Basic equipment; note the Bronze Age replica urn-style pottery vessels (Moore Group).

then dropping them into a water vessel. In a brewing context this process became known in Germany as '*stein beer*' (stone beer). Indeed, up until recently Rauchenfels Brewery in Marktoberdorf, Bavaria, revived this tradition by using heated graywacke to make their own distinctive beer. This dark sandstone resists shattering under the stress of superheating and is quick to cool—ideal for brewing. A beer reviewer had this to say about their product:

> 'The use of stones imparts wonderfully smoky, toffeeish notes to Steinbrau. When the hot rocks are added to the brew kettle (which is made from metal these days), some of the malt sugars will be caramelized right onto the stone surface. The stones, heated in a beechwood fire, will impart their own smokiness to the beer.'

Our first brewing experiment was carried out at Billy's home in Headford, Co. Galway, in August 2007. In an effort to make the experiment authentic, the equipment had to be basic. For the mash tun we used an old, leaky, wooden cattle trough that measured 1.7 m in length, 0.7 m in width and 0.65 m in depth (roughly consistent with the average trough dimensions from excavated *fulachta fiadh*). To make the trough watertight the seams were

Illus. 4—Heating water in the trough with fired rocks in Billy Quinn's backyard brewery (Moore Group).

caulked with moss, a technique used by Bronze Age boat-builders. The trough was then lowered into a ready-made pit and the edges backfilled. Water was then added. Despite some initial leakage, the water in the trough eventually reached a natural level by simply flooding the immediate area. When filled to a depth of 0.55 m, the trough held 350 l.

In choosing the stones for heating we consciously avoided limestone, as most *fulachta fiadh* are made up of non-limestone material. As O'Kelly (1954, 122) observed, heated limestone on contact with water turns to calcium hydroxide, known as 'milk of lime', and is dangerous to ingest. Interestingly, during excavations at Dún Aenghus on the Aran Islands, which geologically is a natural extension of the Burren, a trough was discovered with burnt granite cobbles scattered roundabout (Cotter 1993, 13). Given the lack of granite on the island, these ancient people obviously went to a lot of trouble to source this stone, either by breaking up glacial erratics or by travelling by boat to south Connemara. For the purposes of our experiment we used a mix of granite and sandstone from Clonbur, Co. Galway.

For our Bronze Age brewer, stage one in the process after harvesting and winnowing the barley crop would have involved artificially promoting growth by placing the grain in a textile bag or perforated leather container within a stream, allowing the grains to saturate and swell. This would result in the growth of a sprout or 'acrospire', visible as a rootlet at the base of the grain. At this point the grain is stunted by drying and rolling the grain in hot stones to make a starch-rich, roasted malted barley. The malt is then ready for grinding. In prehistoric times this would have been done with a saddle or rotary quern (grain that has been malted is far more suitable for grinding than unmalted grain, which would still have a water content). Our malted barley (50 kg) was provided by Aidan Murphy, a master brewer with the Galway Hooker Brewing Company. The barley arrived unmilled, and for reasons of convenience and expediency we crushed it using an electrical food-processor. Aidan also supplied us with wet yeast from his brewery. If time had permitted we could have made a simple yeast by kneading a hole in some dough, adding water and leaving it exposed, resulting in the formation of a yeast cake. Yeast is notoriously volatile, however, and we were content to use a known species.

These ancient 'wild' beers would have been spontaneously fermented by particular combinations of local wild yeasts and micro-organisms, as well as local plant and herb flavourings. In all likelihood they may have been somewhat tart, sour and acidic in taste, more like the Lambic beers of Belgium or contemporary Flanders red brown ales (Sparrow 2005, 5).

Echoing the role of airborne yeast, the Norse sagas have it that Odin (the chief god in Norse paganism) disguised himself as an eagle and spilled the secret of beer from the sky (www.beerhunter.com/documents/19133-000103.html, accessed April 2007). Furthermore, in Scandinavia and the Orkneys there is a tradition that early brewers realised that by reusing a stick with which they had stirred previous brews they could activate fermentation in subsequent worts; such sticks thus became valued items, and it was not uncommon for them to be willed from one generation to the next. One can imagine that

Illus. 5—Mashing the malted barley through a wicker basket (Moore Group).

Clockwise from top left:

Illus. 6—Adding occasional heated stones while stirring the wort (Moore Group).

Illus. 7—The finished wort and spent grain (Moore Group).

Illus. 8—Decanting the wort into fermentation vessels (Moore Group).

in prehistoric times these 'wands' impregnated with living yeast cells would have been invested with a spiritual potency.

To begin brewing our prehistoric beer, stones were heated in a wood fire for roughly two hours until superheated before being transferred into the water trough (Illus. 4). After 15–20 minutes we achieved our optimum temperature of 60–70°C. This temperature can be identified by observing the surface of the water. As the water heats it becomes thinner and gently steams, becoming glassy and mirror-still. The ideal temperature is when the reflection is clearest. At this point we half-submerged a wicker basket in the trough and began adding our barley and stirring it vigorously (Illus. 5). Over a period of 45 minutes, maintaining a fairly constant temperature with the addition of occasional heated stones, our water transformed into a sweet-smelling, syrupy wort (Illus. 6 & 7). Even at this stage the nutritional value of the beverage was obvious. If we had decided to add milk, the resultant concoction would be similar to modern-day Horlicks or could have been served as gruel.

After completing the conversion of starches to sugar, ascertained by tasting the wort, we brought the mixture to a boil and then decanted it into fermentation vessels (Illus. 8). We used plastic containers with a total capacity of 75 l. In later experiments we used two Bronze Age replica urn-style pottery vessels, each with a capacity of 30 l. The containers were then cooled in a bath of cold water before we added 350 ml of wet yeast. To counter the sweetness of the wort and lend the beer a more recognisable bitter taste, we added seasonal flavourings sourced near Billy's house. These included sprigs of bog myrtle, juniper berries and yarrow, wrapped in muslin and suspended in the wort. Within eight to nine hours after cooling, the wort audibly began to bubble. Fermentation took place over the course of a week before the beer was ready for bottling. The end result was a relatively clear, copper-coloured brew (Illus. 9), with a sharp yet sweet taste. The hot rocks had imparted a slightly smoky caramelised flavour, making it eminently drinkable. Friends and family likened it to wheat beer and compared it favourably to home-kit brews.

Our beer could best be described as a gruit ale, an old-fashioned herb mixture used for bittering and flavouring beer, popular before the extensive use of hops.

We discovered that the process of brewing beer in a *fulacht fiadh* using hot-rock technology was entirely feasible. The production took only a few hours, followed by a week for fermentation. Three hundred litres of water was transformed into a very palatable 110 l of ale with minimal effort. The spent grain provided the ingredients for a dozen malt loaves (Illus. 10) and the rest was used as cattle fodder. Other than the shattered stone and the remains of the fire, there was little detritus.

Conclusion

So, what is the evidence for brewing? First, the experiment worked. Fermentation caused by wind-blown yeast even occurred in the leftover mash in the trough within a few hours. Secondly, a number of quern-stones have been found in association with *fulachta fiadh* (e.g. Hegarty 2005), indicating that grain-processing was taking place nearby. Furthermore, the fact that hot-rock brewing was carried out to an industrial level until the early part of the last century testifies to the efficiency of the process.

But what of the physical evidence? Should not excavated *fulachta fiadh* contain archaeobotanical remains indicative of malted barley? It is our contention that the spent

Illus. 9—The authors enjoying the fruits (Moore Group).

Illus. 10—A malt loaf being made from the spent grain (Moore Group).

grain, even after mashing, had its uses and would not have been dumped; rather it was treated as a valuable resource and may have been recycled to make bread or, as brewers do to the present day, given to animals as fodder.

The grain normally found on archaeological sites is usually charred and survives owing to its carbonised state, which makes it less susceptible to decay. Charred grain has no nutritional value and certainly has no place in brewing as it would spoil a beer mash.

Ordinary malted grain after mashing is reduced to a non-starchy material consisting of a cellulose pulp comprising the hull and pericarp (the tissue around the seeds). This pulp still contains sugar residues and, given its de-natured state and its high water content, is more vulnerable to microbiological decay if left exposed to the elements. In the archaeological record, given the time-frame, this evidence would be entirely ephemeral. Indeed, our own experience in dumping spent grain in Billy's backyard, although hardly scientific, was telling—within a matter of three months the dumped grain (approximately 125 kg) had disappeared and it was practically impossible to determine the exact dumping spot. The spent grain was eaten by animals, birds or vermin or simply decayed.

In conclusion, beer at its most basic is fermented liquid bread and is a highly nutritious beverage. Our ancestors would have consumed ale on a daily basis as a healthy, uncontaminated, comfort drink. But this does not preclude the fact that in the long Bronze Age evenings and nights, family groups likely sat around a blazing fire telling tales, interacting socially and enjoying the sense of well-being and genial companionship that ale enhances. We suggest that the *fulacht fiadh* was possibly multifunctional, the kitchen sink of the Bronze Age, with many conceivable uses. For us, however, a primary use seems clear: these sites were Bronze Age micro-breweries.

Acknowledgements

We would like to acknowledge the assistance and advice of Merryn and Graham Dineley, Max Nelson, The Hooker Brewing Company, Pete Brown, Libby Best and Maree Daffy, Moore Group and everyone else who helped.

6. Hair of the dog: evidence of early medieval food production and feasting at Ballyvass, Co. Kildare

Tara Doyle

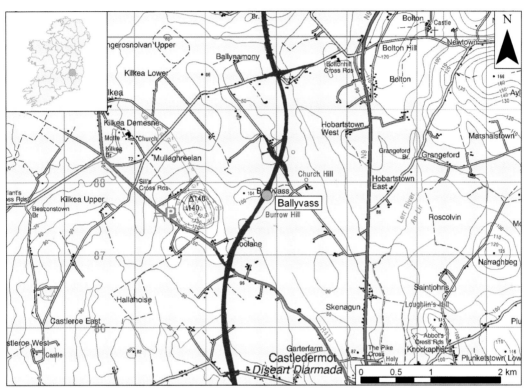

Illus. 1—Location of Ballyvass, Co. Kildare (based on the Ordnance Survey Ireland map).

This paper provides a preliminary glimpse of a vibrant community who lived and worked in a ringfort in the townland of Ballyvass, Co. Kildare, during the early medieval period. The site at Ballyvass, 2 km north-west of Castledermot, was on a gravel ridge with a southern aspect in an area known as Burrow Hill (Illus. 1). It was surrounded by agricultural land, with a gravel extraction quarry to the north-west. In May 2007 archaeological excavation of this previously unidentified site was undertaken by the author for Headland Archaeology Ltd, on behalf of Kildare County Council and the NRA, as part of archaeological works prior to the construction of the N9/N10 Kilcullen–Waterford Scheme: Kilcullen to Carlow.[1]

The elevation of the site offered a panoramic view, extending over several kilometres. Monuments within 1 km of the site included a tumulus (Record of Monuments and Places no. KD038-031), a ringfort (KD038-036), a church site (KD038-037) and a rectangular enclosure (KD038-041); all could be seen from the interior of the enclosure. Another known site, classified as a miscellaneous site (KD038-062), was located directly south-east of the Ballyvass ringfort but was not visible on the ground during the excavation.

55

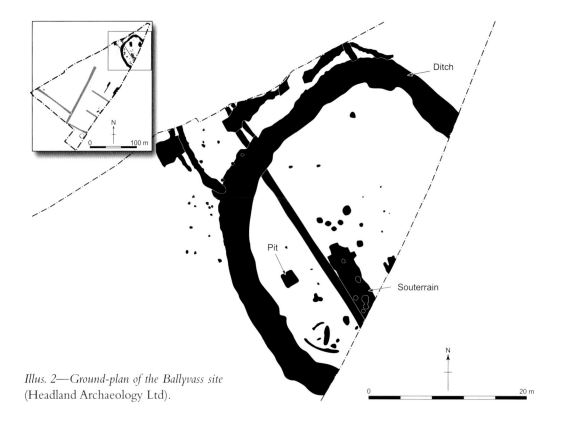

Illus. 2—Ground-plan of the Ballyvass site (Headland Archaeology Ltd).

Ringfort

Excavation revealed approximately 75% of a ditched enclosure located in the north-east corner of the excavation area (Illus. 2). The ditch had a generally V-shaped profile and was on average 3.5 m wide and 2 m deep, with an external diameter of 38 m. Cattle bone from a basal deposit within the ditch returned a radiocarbon date of AD 660–810 (Beta-243988; see Appendix 1 for details of radiocarbon dating results). This date would place the site in the early medieval period, and the enclosure can be classified as a ringfort, of which there are approximately 45,000 known in Ireland (Stout 1997, 53). Two bone pins were recovered from the middle fills of the ditch and sherds of late medieval pottery were identified in the uppermost fills.

No archaeological features were identified in the eastern and north-eastern portions of the enclosure's interior. To the west and south-west several post-holes and pits were located. A medieval swivel knife and a corroded iron fragment were recovered from an oval pit in this area. The largest and most impressive feature within the interior was a large, rectangular, earth-cut trench that measured 11 m long by 3.5 m wide. It ran in a north-west–south-east direction and was located to the south of the enclosure. The eastern and western sides of this trench were vertical and the base was located at a depth of 3.5 m. A terminal at the northern end was slightly rounded, with three plank-slots that were 0.5 m in depth. The exact length of the feature could not be ascertained as it continued into the adjacent field, outside the boundary of the proposed road (Illus. 3).

At least four phases of activity were identified within this feature. The primary function of the trench is uncertain. It is possible that the initial intention was to create a souterrain,

Illus. 3—Elevated view of the site at Ballyvass during excavation, from the west (AirShots Ltd).

or underground passage, to provide a refuge or a storage area. A number of earth-cut, timber-built souterrains are known (Clinton 2001) and this appears to be the most likely interpretation of the trench. Although there was no timber remaining, the vertical walls would have been secured by planks. Evidence of this was provided by thin lines of vertical discolouration on a south-facing section wall. There was no evidence for the use of stone within the souterrain, although this cannot be entirely ruled out as it was not uncommon for building materials to be removed and reused.

Cereal-drying kiln

The secondary use of the souterrain provided a great deal of evidence for the way cereal-processing was conducted in early medieval Ireland. At the northern end of the passage were the burnt remains of a timber-built cereal-drying kiln. The structure was built on a sloping ledge or platform near the base (Illus. 4) and it is possible that the original passage was extended slightly at the northern end to create a platform for the kiln, but at present this hypothesis is unproven. The kiln structure was square in plan and may have been a single- or multi-storey structure, with a flue emerging at a lower level. This form of kiln may be of the tobacco-pipe type (Monk & Kelleher 2005). These kiln types were often constructed against ditches and banks to provide shelter from the elements (ibid.); therefore, a kiln built against the side of an existing trench represents a logical reuse of an abandoned or redundant feature. The importance of drying kilns to the local economy during the early

Illus. 4—Charred remains of the kiln structure during excavation (Headland Archaeology Ltd).

medieval period cannot be underestimated. Until their introduction, drying crops in our damp, wet climate was extremely difficult. A season's harvest could rot if the crop was left in damp conditions for too long, and drying cereal grains as quickly as possible was therefore an important part of crop-processing, unless the crop was to be malted prior to beer production. In the latter case the grain was soaked for a few days and then laid out to dry or placed in a kiln. (For a fuller discussion of cereal-drying kilns see Long, this volume.)

The majority of drying kilns excavated by archaeologists in Ireland are of the keyhole shape, L-shape and figure-of-eight or dumb-bell shape (Monk & Kelleher 2005, 80; Long, this volume). Many are small, shallow features, possibly used once to dry out a single harvest. The drying process at the kiln at Ballyvass would have started at the flue mouth, where a fire was lit. The heat from the fire would travel through a flue funnel and enter into the base of the drying chamber, where the heat would rise into an overhead drying platform or rack. In recent times damp cereals would often have been placed on a bed of straw or linen and spread on a rack or hurdle (Evans 1957, 122–3). This was done carefully to prevent the loss of grain and encourage even drying. Traces of charred linen textile and straw were mixed with the grain in the Ballyvass kiln (Illus. 5). Access to the drying chamber was possibly through a removable roof, hatch or small door. Evidence of a possible roof was indicated by a small clump of charred thatching in the upper contents of the burnt material. The drying process would require constant supervision by an experienced kiln operator. If the fire was left to burn unsupervised the kiln could easily catch fire, as might have happened with this particular kiln at Ballyvass.

A further remarkable discovery was located in part of the flue funnel. This was a shallow, stone-lined pit, with the remains of an adolescent cat curled up at the base. The domestic

Illus. 5—Evidence of (clockwise from left) charred barley grains, straw and linen from the kiln structure at Ballyvass (Headland Archaeology Ltd).

cat was considered economically important to cereal food production in early medieval and medieval Ireland. Cats are recorded in several law-texts of the period and were considered essential to the daily routine of a working kiln or household. Their sole purpose was to keep the grain store or kiln free of mice. The cat of the kiln was said to have the name *cruibne* or 'little paws', and it was written that a cat was worth three cows if it was able to purr and to guard the barn, mill and cereal-drying kiln against mice (Kelly 2000, 243).

Preliminary analysis of cereal grain recovered from the kiln at Ballyvass identified barley (K Stewart, pers. comm.). In early medieval and medieval Ireland, barley was a commonly grown crop, with six-row barley more abundant than the two- or four-row varieties (Monk 1991, 317). A text produced in the eighth century listed the seven most important cereal grains. The ultimate grain and top of the list was bread wheat, which was reserved for the higher-ranking person. Fourth on the list was two-row barley, with six-row barley trailing at fifth place. Bottom of the list was oat cereal, which was considered suitable for the lower-ranking field labourer (Kelly 2000, 226).

Full analysis of the barley grain recovered from the kiln at Ballyvass has yet to be carried out, and the grain may have been grown for bread-making, animal feed or beer-making. A popular use for barley grain during the medieval period was as the main ingredient for beer production. Beer-drinking crossed all social ranks, and beer was consumed by the whole community at feasts and festivals. It was often given to the sick and young for its nutritional properties and was drunk quite often in the absence of clean water. The first documentary sources concerning European drinking habits originate from observations by Roman historians on Germanic tribes around the first century AD:

Illus. 6—North-facing section of the souterrain passage, showing some of the small, later refuse pits and deposits (darker-coloured soils) near the surface (Headland Archaeology Ltd).

'. . . to pass the entire day and night drinking disgraces no one. Their quarrels, as might be expected with intoxicated people, are seldom fought out with mere abuse, but commonly with wounds and bloodshed. Yet, it is at their feasts that they generally consult on the reconciliation of enemies, on matrimonial alliances, on their choice of chiefs, finally even on peace and war, for they think that at no other time is the mind more open to simplicity of purpose or more warmed to noble aspirations' (Tacitus, *Germania*, XXII; translation from Church & Brodribb 1877).

The social customs of beer-drinking were also well commented on in early Irish sources: a law-text on status stipulated that a lord or king was expected not only to provide beer but also to drink it with his household on Sunday; if beer was not provided he was not considered a fair and generous person (Kelly 2000, 332). The container in which the beer was served was also well considered: alcohol served in a horn was thought to be a mark of status (Ward 2006, 5).

As mentioned above, four phases of activity were identified within the souterrain passage. The third phase occurred directly after the destruction of the kiln. This involved a process of natural silting, south of the charred kiln structure, and would have taken place over a short period of time.

The fourth and final phase involved the deposition of organic refuse, and this served to raise the open trench to ground level. A number of smaller pits truncated both the refuse layer and the layer of silting beneath. These pits, mostly located to the south of the passage, were filled with further refuse material (Illus. 6). Many artefacts were recovered from the upper phase, including worked and polished bone, bone pins, corroded fragments of metal, a metal arrowhead and the head of a brooch-pin.

Drinking-horn terminal

The most significant artefact from the ringfort at Ballyvass was recovered from the organic-rich fill at the base of one of the refuse pits. The artefact is a copper-alloy zoomorphic, or animal-like, drinking-horn terminal mount (Illus. 7). A radiocarbon date of AD 770–980 (Beta-243989) was obtained from charred barley grain surrounding the object.

Dr Carol Neuman de Vegvar of Ohio Wesleyan University is currently compiling a catalogue of multi-period drinking-horn terminal mounts from Ireland and Europe. To date, 14 terminal mounts have been found in Ireland (C Neuman de Vegvar, pers. comm.). The mount would have been attached to the tapered point of a relatively small animal horn and a rivet would have held it securely in place. Resin is often found inside the mount and was used as a glue to secure the metal to the horn (ibid.). The Ballyvass mount would have been attached to a short horn similar to that of a cow (Illus. 8). Many examples of drinking-horns from Europe are found with a metal mount attached to the rim and point, and occasionally a smaller metal mount is located midway down the horn. This was used in conjunction with a cord or chain from which to hang the horn when not in use (ibid.). No evidence for horn mount fragments was identified among the other artefacts recovered in similar deposits on the Ballyvass site.

The most famous Irish drinking-horn is the Kavanagh 'Charter' Horn, a ceremonial drinking-horn of elephant ivory dating from the early 12th century, with brass mountings added in the 15th century. It was owned by the MacMorrough Kavanagh kings of Leinster for centuries, and at present resides in the National Museum of Ireland (Ó Floinn 1991).

The customs surrounding the drinking-horn in Ireland are mostly speculative, fragmented stories surviving through folklore and texts, including stories like 'The three drinking horns of Cormac úa Cuinn' (Gwynn 1905). Images of feasting and of drinking from a horn are found in works of art like the Bayeaux Tapestry in France or the stone and metal sculptures of the drinking-horn bearers of the so-called 'valkyrie amulets' from Scandinavia (Ward 2006, 9), where drinking-horn customs are also well documented. One common ceremony, known as *simbel*, involved the formal presentation of a horn or cup to the king or lord of the hall by the highest-ranking woman present. This token would confirm the king's dominance and rulership among the gathering. The horn would then be passed round amongst the rest of the participants in order of rank. The sharing of the cup helped to establish a bond between all ranking men, forming a tribal band of brothers. The one holding the horn or cup would make a toast, an oath or a boast, and on occasion might sing a song or recite a poem before passing the cup along.

0 1 cm

Illus. 7—The Ballyvass drinking-horn terminal mount (John Sunderland).

Illus. 8 (below)—Artistic impression of a drinking-horn, illustrating where the Ballyvass terminal mount was attached to the horn (Sara Nylund).

Illus. 9—Detail of the head on the Ballyvass drinking-horn mount (John Sunderland).

The zoomorphic image on the Ballyvass terminal mount represents a simplistic recognisable image of a dog or hound (Illus. 9). Animal imagery was commonly used in northern European art of the early medieval period (Edwards 1990, 133). Often the image represented a bird, ox or mythical beast. It is not surprising that an image of a dog was used on a terminal mount to decorate an Irish drinking-horn. Irish common laws of the Early Christian period show that the dog was revered as an important member of a household and performed specific tasks like guarding, hunting or herding. The most revered dog of all was the guard dog, often referred to as a 'slaughter hound' or 'a dog of four doors'. The owners of these fierce dogs were considered to be the élite among society. The four doors are a reference to the master's house, the sheepfold and the byres of the calves and oxen. Anyone who killed such a guard dog was to give 10 cows to the owner and replace the dead animal with a dog of the same breed (Kelly 2000, 114–16). The superior breeding and training afforded to Irish dogs were noted on the Continent, where a story praises the skill of an Irish dog that was able to divide a mixed herd of cattle into two groups on the basis of their markings. The dog, Vigi, had been given by its Irish owner to a Norse king (Monsen 1932, 139).

Conclusion

The excavations carried out in advance of this new section of the N9/N10 resulted in a wealth of information regarding the everyday existence of people living and working in the area during the early medieval period. The presence of a cereal-drying kiln indicates that cereal-processing was taking place at the Ballyvass ringfort. Barley was the grain identified within the kiln and its uses are documented in the law-texts and annals of the time.

Although beer production may not have been the only use made of the dried barley grain, the chances are that some of it would have been fermented to drink on special occasions like feasts or festivals. This theory is also supported by the recovery of the drinking-horn terminal mount, discarded or lost among the refuse from a nearby homestead.

We can only speculate about the importance placed on the drinking-horn and the customs involved at such gatherings. Documentary sources from the Continent enlighten us as to the attitude to drink and the customs involved. It is not unreasonable to suggest that similar customs may have been practised on some scale on this island. The image of the hound used on the drinking-horn terminal mount supports the documentary evidence for dogs having played a significant role in Irish society at the time, such that it warranted being immortalised on an object of great social importance. The evidence from this excavation shows that cats and dogs made valued contributions to the early medieval community of Ballyvass.

The archaeological evidence indicates that a vibrant agricultural community once thrived in the area. There is no evidence to suggest that a farmstead existed within the excavated part of the ringfort at Ballyvass, although it is possible that additional evidence may exist in the unexcavated portion or at the ringfort (KD038-036) located 350 m to the east. What we can be certain of is that crop-processing, and possibly the activities deriving from it, was familiar to the people living and working in the immediate area of Ballyvass.

Acknowledgements

I wish to thank NRA Archaeologist Noel Dunne and all the excavation team and staff at Headland Archaeology Ltd for their support and advice. Thanks also to Dr Carol Neuman de Vegvar for her comments on the zoomorphic drinking-horn terminal mount; to Elizabeth Heckett for her preliminary analysis of the textile; to Sara Nylund for the reconstruction drawing of the drinking-horn terminal mount; and to John Sunderland for the photographs of the terminal mount.

Note

1. NGR 276870, 187816; height 96–8 m OD; excavation reg. no. E2996; ministerial direction no. A021.

7. To the waters and the wild: ancient hunting in County Kildare

Patricia Long and Gillian McCarthy

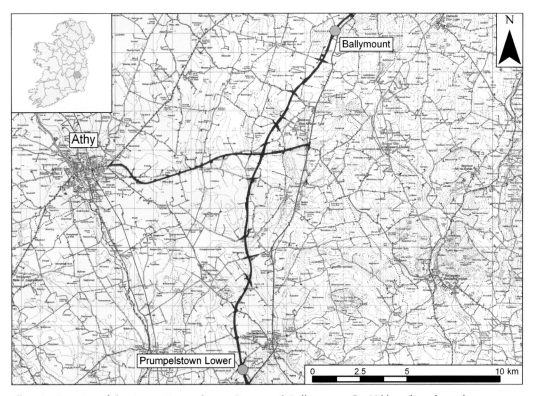

Illus. 1—Location of the sites at Prumpelstown Lower and Ballymount, Co. Kildare (based on the Ordnance Survey Ireland map).

Wild animals, birds and fish have been exploited by humans from the time they first settled on this island up to the present day. While animal bone analysis can determine what species were being used, it tells us little about how these animals were actually procured. Early medieval documents describe a number of techniques for hunting deer and wild pig, including chasing them with hounds, ambushing or trapping them, stunning them with a heavy log, or driving them into a net, barrier, stake or pit (Kelly 2000; pers. comm.). Physical evidence of these techniques is relatively rare on archaeological sites, but finds made during two excavations in advance of the N9/N10 Kilcullen–Waterford Scheme: Kilcullen to Carlow provided an insight into some of the hunting methods employed by the inhabitants of that area. The excavations were undertaken by Headland Archaeology Ltd on behalf of Kildare County Council and the NRA.

Wooden artefacts from a river floodplain

Extensive excavations were undertaken on either side of the River Lerr, near Castledermot, Co. Kildare (Illus. 1). The archaeological remains uncovered dated from as early as the

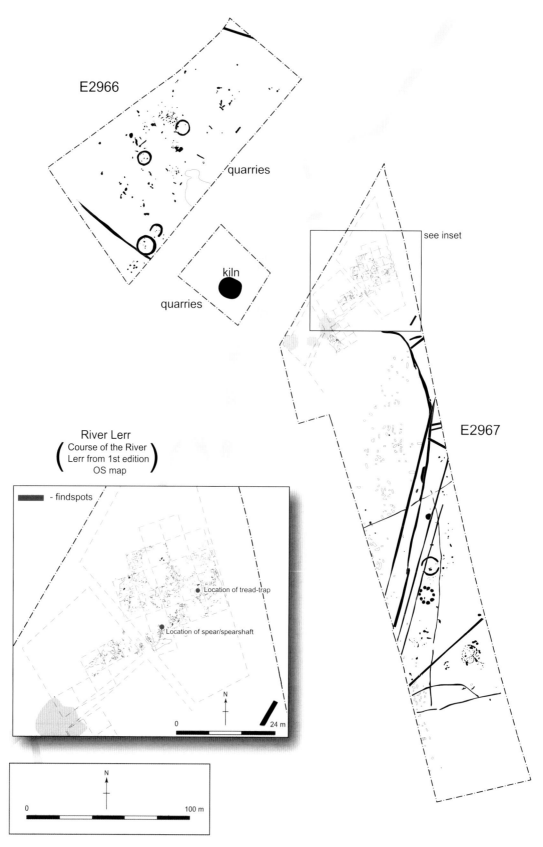

Illus. 2—Plan of the excavated features at Prumpelstown Lower (south of the River Lerr) and Woodlands West (north of the river), indicating the find-spots of the tread-trap and the spear/spearshaft in the floodplain (Headland Archaeology Ltd).

Illus. 3—The tread-trap during excavation (Headland Archaeology Ltd).

Mesolithic period, with phases of activity continuing into the post-medieval period. Included in the excavation was part of the river floodplain, in the townland of Prumpelstown Lower.[1] A series of wooden trackways were identified in the floodplain as well as three burnt mounds. It was also in this area that tangible evidence of hunting activity was recovered in the form of two wooden artefacts (Illus. 2).

The first was an animal trap, found at the base of a peat deposit that was 0.4 m deep (Illus. 3). It consisted of two movable oak panels (known as valves), which slotted into a rectangular oak frame with a central bevelled opening. A lattice of 'teeth' made from animal bone was inserted into the edges of the valves. Two horizontal holes were bored into either end of the frame and fragments of hazel rods were found within these. There were also two vertical holes at one end of the frame, with linear grooves between them (Illus. 4). These grooves appear to be the impression of some kind of rope, the purpose of which is as yet unclear, but possibilities include repairing the large crack evident on the frame or tethering the trap while it was in use.

The characteristics of this trap are typical of a group of artefacts known as tread-traps (Stephens 1996). There are 23 of these traps known in Ireland, two in Britain and at least

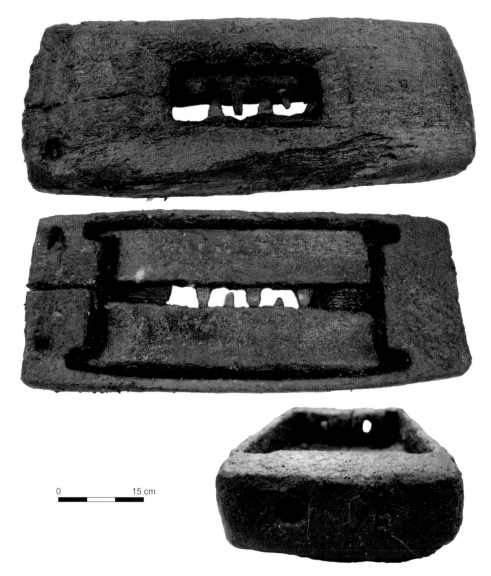

0 _____ 15 cm

Illus. 4—Views of the top, bottom and side of the tread-trap (Headland Archaeology Ltd).

40 from southern Scandinavia and Central Europe (ibid.). The Irish examples are concentrated mainly in the north and west, and they occur individually except for a group of nine traps from Larkhill, Co. Fermanagh (Allingham 1896).

Tread-traps can have either one or two valves, and the Prumpelstown Lower trap is the first bivalvular trap to be discovered in Britain or Ireland. It is also the first trap found in this region with teeth inserted in the valve edges. Wooden teeth are known from Continental European examples but no other tread-trap is known to have bone teeth.

Over the years many theories have been put forward regarding the purpose and mechanism of tread-traps. A combination of experiments using models of archaeological traps (Graham-Smith 1923; Stephens 1996) and ethnographic research in Poland and Russia (Moszynski 1929) have suggested that they were set in pits in the ground and were intended to trap the leg of a passing animal. In general, tread-traps are oblong and on average 1000 mm in length, with channels and pegs used to hold flexible pieces of wood to spring the trap; the Prumpelstown Lower trap, however, was shorter (650 mm), rectangular and without channels.

In the case of bivalvular traps, two springs were used and the valves forced open and held apart by a tripping board (Stephens 1996). Two horizontal holes were bored into either end of the Prumpelstown Lower trap and it is suggested that these were used to hold the springs, which would have consisted of hazel rods passed through the holes across the opening in the frame. The valves were then forced open against these springs and held in place by a tripping board. The set trap is likely to have been placed in a pit with the central opening in the frame facing upwards. The leg of a passing animal, on entering the opening, would have dislodged the board and the valves would have snapped shut, trapping the animal.

While the intended quarry of this particular trap is difficult to determine, it seems likely to have been red deer. Red deer bones were the only wild animal remains identified in the floodplain deposits at Prumpelstown Lower (A Tourunen, pers. comm.). Ethnographic research found that tread-traps in Europe were predominantly used to hunt deer (Stephens 1996), though smaller mammals were also targeted. Other evidence to suggest that tread-traps were used for hunting deer in Ireland is found in the form of carvings on an early medieval grave-slab at Clonmacnoise, Co. Offaly (Munro & Gillespie 1919), and on a high cross at Banagher, Co. Offaly (Soderberg 2004), which show a deer being trapped by the hind leg in what appears to be a tread-trap.

The setting of traps of this type to catch deer may also be implied by some early medieval law-texts that refer to a pierced board (*clár toll*) in association with a deer-pit (*cuitheach*) (Kelly 2000, 279). Water-filled *cuitheach* are also mentioned in the texts (ibid.). This may have served to disguise the trap close to a watering-hole and would have naturally occurred in the floodplain at Prumpelstown Lower.

A broad date range has been suggested for these traps (Stephens 1996). Pollen dating has suggested Middle Bronze Age and Iron Age dates for Scandinavian examples and a Late Bronze Age date for a trap from Drummacaladdery, Co. Donegal (Mitchell 1945, 16). More recently a Scottish example from Aberdeenshire has been radiocarbon-dated to AD 530–680 (Sheridan 2005, 21), and one of the Larkhill traps was dated to the mid-sixth century AD (Stephens 1996, 62). The Prumpelstown Lower trap has yet to be scientifically dated. Initial analysis of the woodworking technology suggests that metal tools were used to make the trap (E OCarroll, pers. comm.).

The second wooden artefact found in the floodplain was a pointed length of yew brushwood (Illus. 5). Initial analysis of this object has suggested that it may have been a spear or a spearshaft. It measured 1,905 mm in length and was circular in cross-section with a maximum diameter of 25 mm at the pointed end, tapering to 6 mm at the other end. Branches had been trimmed along its length and the point was very finely worked (E

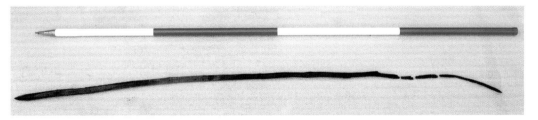

Illus. 5—The spear/spearshaft (Headland Archaeology Ltd).

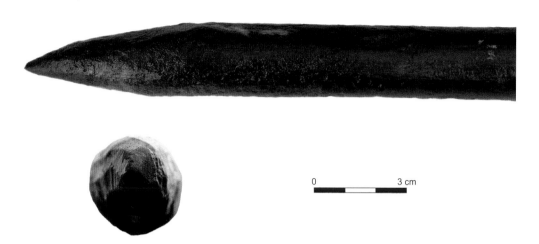

Illus. 6—Detail of the pointed end of the spear/spearshaft (Headland Archaeology Ltd).

OCarroll, pers. comm.) (Illus. 6). Two very similar pointed yew objects recovered beneath an Iron Age trackway in bogland at Edercloon, Co. Longford, have been interpreted as spearshafts (Moore 2007; 2008, 8; pers. comm.); the absence of any evidence for the hafting of a spearhead on the Prumpelstown Lower object and the fine nature of the point suggest, however, that it may have been functional in its own right. Further expert analysis will determine a date for the object and allow more definitive comment on its function.

Pit-trap

The second site where evidence of animal-trapping was identified was at Ballymount, Co. Kildare, on the edge of Narraghmore Bog.[2] A pit-trap was located here in close proximity to several burnt mound deposits, a rectangular trough, several small pits and a sunken, circular, stone-lined feature. The pit itself measured 4.6 m east–west, 2.8 m north–south and 0.9 m. The most notable thing about this pit was that 16 stake-holes were identified on the steeply sloping sides. The inclination of the stake-holes implied that all the stakes were pointing inwards and towards one end of the feature (Illus. 7); this has led to the interpretation of the feature as a pit-trap. This trap would have been hidden deliberately in undergrowth and prey would have been driven into it and become impaled on sharpened wooden stakes (Illus. 8). Bone from both red deer and pig was recovered from the vicinity of the pit during the excavation, indicating that these animals might have fallen victim to the pit-trap. The proximity of the pit-trap to a burnt mound would point to a prehistoric date but scientific dating will confirm whether this is the case.

Conclusion

These sites have given a fascinating glimpse into ancient hunting techniques in south-east Ireland. Although still in the early stages of post-excavation analysis, they have demonstrated that people were exploiting wild resources, which would have been abundant on the banks

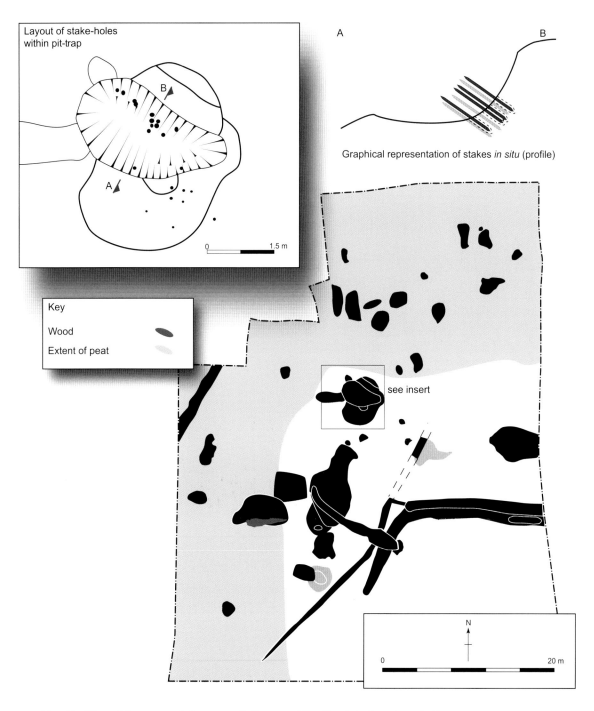

Layout of stake-holes within pit-trap

A — B

Graphical representation of stakes *in situ* (profile)

Key

Wood

Extent of peat

0   1.5 m

see insert

N

0   20 m

Illus. 7—Plan of the excavated features at Ballymount (Headland Archaeology Ltd).

of the River Lerr and on the edge of Narraghmore Bog. The effort and skill that went into the hunting techniques described above would suggest that it was a specialised activity, which, as well as a means of obtaining food and raw material, might have been a sport or even a route to improved social standing for the hunter.

Illus. 8—A reconstruction drawing of how the pit-trap might have been used (Eavan O'Dochartaigh, Headland Archaeology Ltd).

Acknowledgements

Thanks are due to all those who contributed to the excavation and post-excavation work related to the sites mentioned above, in particular NRA Archaeologist Noel Dunne and our colleagues at Headland Archaeology Ltd: Colm Moloney (senior archaeologist), Maura O'Malley, Lyndsey Clark and Rob Hanbidge (site supervisors), Eavan O'Dochartaigh (illustrator) and the graphics department, Auli Tourunen (zooarchaeologist), and Jean Price and Damian Shiels for editing drafts of this paper. Thanks also to Fergus Kelly, Caitríona Moore and Alison Sheridan for sharing unpublished information, and to Ellen OCarroll, who carried out the wood species identifications and commented on the wooden artefacts.

Notes

1. Prumpelstown Lower: NGR 276696, 183723; height 67.81 m OD; excavation reg. no. E2967; ministerial direction no. A021; excavation director Patricia Long.
2. Ballymount: NGR 281581, 201100; height 106 m OD; excavation reg. no. E2874; ministerial direction number A021; excavation director Gillian McCarthy.

8. Excavating a meal: a multidisciplinary approach to early medieval food economy

Alison Kyle, Karen Stewart and Auli Tourunen

Illus. 1—Location of the sites discussed in this paper (Headland Archaeology Ltd).

The early medieval period is one for which we have an abundance of archaeological and historical evidence, which has increased in recent years as a result of the national roads-building programme. This has led to a wealth of information that benefits research in all sectors of the archaeological profession. It is now possible to synthesise these data by taking a holistic approach, integrating the work of individual specialties.

The Specialist Services Department within Headland Archaeology Ltd includes the current authors: Alison Kyle (finds specialist), Karen Stewart (archaeobotanist) and Auli Tourunen (faunal remains specialist). The authors are ideally placed to take a multidisciplinary approach to the data gathered during an excavation, facilitating an integrated interpretation of the site.

Material evidence from four early medieval sites is referred to throughout this paper (Illus. 1); these were generally low-status settlement sites where a range of activities took place, including, in one instance, burial (see Appendix 1 for radiocarbon dating results). Kilcloghans, Co. Galway, was a univallate ringfort, excavated in 2007 under the direction of Liam McKinstry on the route of the N17 Tuam Bypass (McKinstry 2008).[1] Carrowkeel, also in County Galway, was a so-called 'cemetery-settlement' excavated in 2005 by Brendon Wilkins as part of the N6 Galway to East Ballinasloe PPP Scheme (O'Sullivan 2007b,

Illus. 2—Artist's impression of early medieval food economy activity and the landscape (Sara Nylund, Headland Archaeology Ltd).

90–3).[2] A number of early medieval pits and ditches were excavated in the townland of Moyle Big in County Carlow. This site was directed by Joanne Hughes during excavations in 2005–6 that were part of the N9/N10 Kilcullen–Waterford Scheme: Kilcullen to Carlow.[3] Finally, a ringfort at Ballyvass, Co. Kildare, was excavated in 2007 as part of the same road scheme and was directed by Tara Doyle (see this volume). The four excavations were conducted by Headland Archaeology Ltd on behalf of Galway County Council, Kildare County Council and the NRA.

This paper discusses the stages of the early medieval food economy, from production to processing and preparation, and finally to consumption. In a food economy, production can involve the sourcing of food from animal husbandry, crop cultivation and wild resources; processing includes activities that enable these raw materials to be consumed; and consumption refers to the stage at which the products are eaten (Illus. 2).

Production

Production is generally the most archaeologically elusive of the phases with which this analysis deals; both animal husbandry and crop production leave few traces in the archaeological record. Within bone assemblages it is difficult to separate animals bred and slaughtered on the site from animals brought in for slaughter or even as ready-cut pieces. There is some archaeological evidence for the sheltering of livestock (Simpson 1999, 20; Waterman 1972, 31). The presence of lice that live on domestic animals (Kenward & Allison

Illus. 3—Infant pig skull from Kilcloghans, Co. Galway (Headland Archaeology Ltd).

1994, 102) or in layers of manure (Tourunen 2008, 79) also indicate the presence of live animals. Another possible indication is the presence of infant animal bones. These often represent miscarriages, stillbirths or animals that died shortly after birth rather than animals that have been consumed (e.g. O'Connor 1991, 248; 2003, 80). The presence of such bones may therefore indicate that animal-breeding was practised at these sites.

These data must be interpreted carefully, however, as calves may have been slaughtered for the production of vellum (manuscript parchment produced from calfskin). Interestingly, socketed tools with prongs recovered from Kilcloghans may have been used in the processing of cattle hides (Kyle 2008; McKinstry 2008). Only a few infant cattle remains were recovered from Kilcloghans, however, thus the remains might rather represent instances of pregnant animals being slaughtered and the foetuses discarded. At Carrowkeel, Ballyvass and Kilcloghans, however, infant cattle, sheep/goat (sheep and goat cannot always be distinguished based on skeletal evidence) and pig were all identified (Illus. 3). Therefore these bones probably represent animal-breeding taking place in the vicinity of these sites.

Tillage was an important part of the early medieval food economy, as can be seen in the contemporary law-tracts (Kelly 2000), and charred cereal grains are commonly recovered during excavations of early medieval sites (Monk & Kelleher 2005) (Illus. 4). This does not, however, necessarily mean that crops were being grown at the site, as sheaves and processed grain were relatively easy to transport. The presence of cereal pollen is a more definitive indicator of cereal crop cultivation, as the grains of cereal pollen are particularly large (Faegri & Iverson 1975) and tend not to travel far from the plant.

Illus. 4—Oat (left) and barley (right) grains recovered from Kilcloghans, Co. Galway (Headland Archaeology Ltd).

Although there is some evidence from faunal and plant remains for food production, the most direct archaeological evidence for production comes from artefactual assemblages. With regard to tillage, components of ploughs are occasionally found during excavations. These show that the 'heavy plough' was in use in Ireland by the mid-seventh century AD (Ó Cróinín 1995, 91). This type of plough was a technological innovation as it incorporated the use of a mould-board, which meant that ploughs no longer simply cut the sod but also turned it to form ridges and furrows (Mitchell & Ryan 1997, 234). This innovation allowed for an increase in agricultural output.

Sickles that have been recovered from excavated early medieval sites, and those discussed in the written records in the form of the law-texts, provide evidence that early medieval harvesting was somewhat different to the harvesting of today. Instead of cutting crops at the base of the stalks—which would have required the use of a long-bladed sickle known as a scythe—and storing the straw for winter, it is thought that fodder crops were cut close to the ear and the stalks left in the field for grazing (Kelly 2000, 238). It is of note that scythes are as yet unknown from early medieval Irish contexts (ibid., 480). It is possible to infer the conditions in which crops were grown and the season at which crops were harvested from crop weed evidence (Jones et al. 2004), and in the early medieval period crops grew to a greater, and much more variable, height than those of today (Moffet 2006, 47).

Wild animal resources do not seem to have played an important role at Carrowkeel, Ballyvass or Kilcloghans. At Carrowkeel and Kilcloghans, for instance, the number of fish bones proved to be insignificant. The lack of these bones in even finely sieved samples further supports their absence from the economy rather than merely being a product of

Illus. 5—Charred hazelnut shells from Carrowkeel, Co. Galway (Headland Archaeology Ltd).

poor preservation. The Ballyvass analysis is still ongoing but seems to follow the same pattern. The low number of wild animals is a common feature of early medieval animal bone samples (McCormick & Murray 2007, 104).

Palaeoenvironmental samples taken at Kilcloghans and Carrowkeel were found to contain charred hazelnut shells, though in low concentrations in both cases. Hazelnut shells frequently occur on early medieval sites. These are almost always charred (Illus. 5), as carbonisation preserves the shells, which would otherwise rot. It is likely that these nuts were consumed by the inhabitants of the site, though the possibility remains that they may have been accidentally included in a fuel assemblage if hazel wood was being used for firewood.

Preparation and processing

Evidence for crop-processing is more abundant in the archaeological record than evidence for crop cultivation. Settlement sites containing charred grain evidence can be classified as being 'producer' or 'consumer' sites (Hillman 1981; Jones 1985), although there are problems inherent in doing so (van der Veen & Jones 2006). Sites containing high proportions of chaff (that is, the inedible fragments of cultivated grains) and weed seeds might be considered 'producer' sites. Unfortunately, the latter sites are very rare in the archaeological record as these early stages of processing do not usually come into contact with fire, and thus would not be preserved. Cereal-drying kilns are also a common occurrence on or near early medieval sites (Monk & Kelleher 2005). It was in the cereal-drying kilns that cereals came into contact with fire, as fire was used to create the warm air that dried out the grains prior to use or storage. A tobacco-pipe-shaped kiln was excavated at Ballyvass and, though analysis is in the very early stages, considerable quantities of grain were recovered, particularly barley grains, which may be associated with brewing (Doyle, this volume).

Meat preparation can also be seen in the bone evidence; for instance, roasting over an open fire can leave burn marks on bones, such as those present at Kilcloghans, as the ends of the bones sticking out were exposed to fire but the meat protected the rest (McCormick & Murray 2007, 51). Butchery can leave marks on animal bones, although a skilful butcher could cut the carcass without leaving marks on the bones. This was desirable as cutting to the bone could damage or blunt a knife more quickly than through ordinary use. Whetstones, used to sharpen blunted knives, were therefore occasionally necessary in the processing of animal carcasses.

Cut marks on bones can indicate how the carcass was butchered: for example, whether the torso was split in half axially through the spine or whether the bones were separated from joints. The nature of the cut marks varies depending on the type of implement used to carry out the butchery. Axes could be used for the initial stages of butchery, while knives were used for the more skilled or refined aspects of carcass preparation. It is possible that small domestic knives, recovered from both Kilcloghans and Carrowkeel (Franklin 2008), may have been used in the butchery of animals (Illus. 6).

Sexton (1998, 76) notes that there were two main categories of cereal food types in early medieval Ireland: breads and pot-based preparations (which included both porridges and gruels). Quern-stones, which were used to grind cereal to produce flour, were indispensable in the preparation of cereal-based foods and were therefore essential components of domestic life. While there is no evidence of the use of ovens in this period, it has been

Illus. 6—Domestic knife blade from Carrowkeel, Co. Galway (Headland Archaeology Ltd).

Illus. 7—Unconserved bucket hoop from Kilcloghans, Co. Galway (Headland Archaeology Ltd).

suggested that breads may have been cooked in a 'pot-oven': foods would have been placed in a lidded ceramic vessel that would then either have been heated by embers or placed directly in a fire (ibid., 80). The production and use of ceramic vessels, termed Souterrain Ware, in early medieval Ireland was largely restricted to north-east Ulster, however (Ryan 1973; Edwards 1990). Thus it is not likely that pot-ovens were in use over most of the country, if at all. It is possible that breads were cooked on metal griddles or flat stones, which were again either placed directly in the fire or heated by embers (McLaren et al. 2004, 20), the latter leaving little trace in the archaeological record.

Porridges and gruels were undoubtedly prepared over a fire, but the archaeological record can provide further detail on the techniques employed. While the use of domestic ceramic vessels was geographically restricted, Souterrain Ware was encountered during excavations at Moyle Big, Co. Carlow, some distance outside its main distribution zone. Sooting on the external surfaces of sherds from this assemblage indicates that the vessels were used for cooking. Furthermore, residue adhering to the internal surfaces of a number of these sherds represents the carbonised remains of a food that was cooked in these pots. The sooting pattern present on a small number of these sherds indicates that cooking was carried out by placing the vessel directly in the hearth rather than by suspension. This is evidenced by the presence of soot on the vessel walls accompanied by an absence of soot on the base (Rice 1987, 235), which would not have been exposed to soot as it would have been obscured by embers.

While Souterrain Ware was undoubtedly commonly used for cooking, it is also possible that vessels were used for storage, as either a primary or secondary function (Kyle 2007, 79). Metal, wood and leather alternatives would have been used in the absence of ceramics, but organic materials rarely survive in the archaeological record. Excavations at the Kilcloghans ringfort recovered two iron bucket hoops (Illus. 7) and a possible bucket handle. While none of the wooden components of the bucket survived, we can use the presence of these metal objects to infer the presence of a wooden bucket that may have been used to feed livestock, for milking or to store foodstuffs.

Consumption

In the absence of direct evidence for consumption, such as human faeces, we have to make certain assumptions and inferences based on indirect evidence. While primarily a physical necessity, the consumption of food is, in all societies, a social action that both reflects and consolidates social positions (Jones 2007; van der Veen 2003). This seems to have been particularly true in early medieval Ireland. According to the contemporary law-tracts, Irish society was organised in distinctive hierarchical layers based on a client–lord relationship (Gerriets 1983; Kelly 2005, 29–38). This relationship required the lord to provide land, livestock and protection for his clients, and in return his clients were required to pay food rents to the lord. If this was in fact the case, consumption in early medieval Ireland may be said to be two-tiered, with low-level consumption representing the family or household and high-level consumption representing the client–lord relationship, which may have involved aspects of feasting.

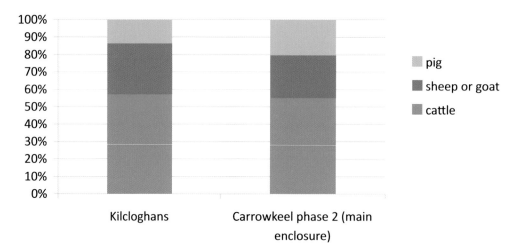

Illus. 8—The proportions of cattle, sheep or goat and pig (Number of Identified Specimens [NISP]) at Kilcloghans and Carrowkeel.

In the written records cattle are valued most highly, while sheep and pigs receive less emphasis (Kelly 2000, 27). This very same emphasis—the domination of cattle, followed by either sheep or pig—can be seen in most of the animal bone assemblages recovered from excavated sites (McCormick & Murray 2007, 104), regardless of the status of their former inhabitants. This might imply that animal husbandry was very static in early medieval Ireland and that the same patterns of production were used at all sites (Illus. 8). Nevertheless, though similar bone assemblages are recovered from different site types, it remains possible that different consumption patterns are present.

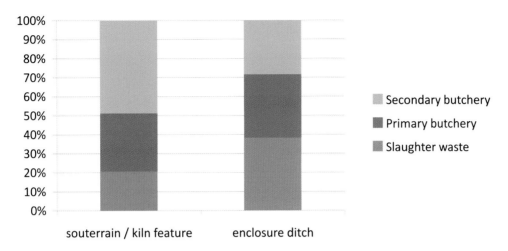

Illus. 9—Differences in the anatomical distribution of cattle (NISP) at Ballyvass, Co. Kildare.

Food rent included both live animals and meat (Kelly 2000, 320). Part of the food rent was likely to be transported into a lord's household for consumption, but one form of food rent involved feasting in the client's household (ibid., 320, 357). The anatomical distribution, i.e. the proportion of different body parts present, created by feasting may be difficult to identify from normal consumption if complete animals were consumed (McCormick 2002, 29–31). This type of feasting in several locations will not create great differences in the animal bone assemblages. Young male animals formed a large part of the food rent (Kelly 2000, 59–62, 72, 87), however, and it might be expected that the bones of these animals were more likely to accumulate at the higher-status settlements, even if mixed with normal household waste. Therefore the age and sex distribution of the consumed animals within the same species might prove to be a useful tool when analysing the social status of the sites.

Plant food consumption was also constrained by social custom. For instance, bread wheat was considered the highest-status cereal, followed by rye, oats, barley and other wheat species, such as spelt and emmer (Kelly 2000, 219). Peas and beans were regarded as having the least status and their cultivation may have been seen as 'women's work' (Ó Corráin 2005, 567).

The grain species distribution at the discussed sites seems to correspond to the status accorded them in the law-tracts. Oats and barley dominate the grain assemblages at these sites, while bread wheat is the least abundant. This seems to reflect the low-status nature of the four sites.

At Kilcloghans a horse bone (pelvis) with cut marks was recovered. According to the historical sources, horseflesh was not consumed during this period (Kelly 2000, 352–3), but it is not yet clear whether this rule was always obeyed (Murray & McCormick 2005, 73). The presence of horse bones does not necessarily indicate horseflesh consumption: horses could have been used for their skin, bones and hair (Rackham 2004, 20–1). Thus cut marks on horse bones might reflect skinning or dismemberment rather than consumption (ibid.). The location of the cut marks on the Kilcloghans horse pelvis—on the surface articulating against the spine—is significant as they relate to dismemberment rather than defleshing for consumption.

At Ballyvass ringfort, evidence of consumption was present in the animal bone material from a possible souterrain, or subterranean passage, within the ringfort, which was reused as a kiln (Doyle, this volume) (Illus. 9). The animal bones from this feature were predominantly food waste, compared with the higher levels of slaughter waste recovered from the enclosure ditch. This difference may reflect spatial differentiation in the activities at the site (see below).

An example of the usefulness of integrating various strands of evidence is apparent at Kilcloghans. The artefactual, archaeobotanical and faunal evidence all indicated domestic activities. The archaeobotanical and faunal evidence, however, indicated a difference in the species present between the enclosure and the souterrain (Illus. 10 & 11).

As can be seen in Illus. 10, the souterrain contained more cattle bones than the enclosure ditch. Also, the souterrain was found to contain evidence of bread wheat, which was absent from the enclosure ditch. Unfortunately, these features date from the same period and their respective chronologies are not clear. Nevertheless, the environmental evidence may allow us to identify a change in the activities at the site even within one archaeological phase. This could be an indication of the dynamic nature of early medieval society. McCormick and Murray (2007, 108–9) have proposed that the decreasing numbers of cattle in archaeological assemblages are linked to the decreasing importance of cattle as a currency as the early medieval period progressed. The accumulation of environmental evidence such as that recovered at Kilcloghans will contribute to our understanding of the social framework of society in the early medieval period. At the moment the evidence for this period in the Galway region, as well as the absence of an absolute chronology at the site, does not allow us to test the data from this site against the model proposed by McCormick and Murray.

Conclusion

The excavations undertaken under the remit of the NRA's policy of archaeological excavation have produced a wealth of evidence relating to the early medieval period. The transects across the landscape that are excavated in advance of road projects produce a less biased sample of the archaeological landscape than the more selective research-led excavations. This allows for the analysis of sites that might otherwise go undetected and unremarked. Environmental evidence is recovered from most excavated early medieval sites; the wider the range of site types excavated, the more we can use these data to build interpretative frameworks for the production, processing, consumption and disposal of foodstuffs in early medieval Ireland. The faunal evidence, for example, is broadly similar across all of the sites discussed, even taking into account their disparate characters, as well as in comparison with larger, higher-status sites such as Knowth (McCormick & Murray 2007). The archaeobotanical evidence is likewise broadly similar, constrained as it is by the limited suite of cereals cultivated during the early medieval period. As discussed above regarding Ballyvass, however, small changes in this record, in association with the historical sources, can tell us a great deal about the inhabitants of the sites. The material culture recovered from ringforts throughout Ireland is generally homogeneous, deriving from the daily domestic tasks that were carried out on occupation sites, regardless of status. In contrast, while such 'mundane' artefacts are found at higher-status sites, prestige items, such

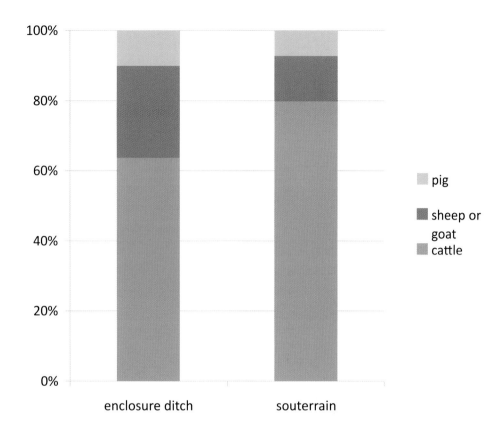

Illus. 10—Species composition of animal bone (NISP) from within the ringfort ditch and the souterrain at Kilcloghans.

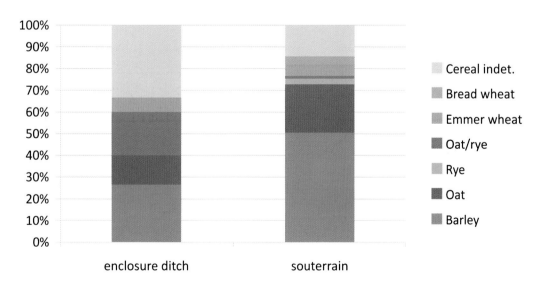

Illus. 11—Species composition of the cereal grains from the ringfort ditch and souterrain at Kilcloghans.

as dress ornaments and objects made from special or rare materials or of unusual form, are frequently recovered. This was the case at Ballyvass (see Doyle, this volume), while only the ubiquitous domestic objects were recovered from Kilcloghans and Carrowkeel.

Environmental and artefactual evidence recovered in the course of these excavations has shed light on the types of food people ate in the early medieval period and the different ways in which that food was prepared and the contexts within which it was consumed. The various strands of evidence—artefactual, archaeobotanical and faunal—allow us to make comparisons not only between sites but also within sites. This allows different interpretations to be tested against multiple classes of evidence, thereby refining our understanding and knowledge of the ways of life of the people who inhabited these sites.

Acknowledgements

We would like to thank the NRA, in particular NRA Assistant Archaeologist Martin Jones and NRA Archaeologists Noel Dunne and Jerry O'Sullivan, Galway County Council, Kildare County Council and Carlow County Council. We are also grateful to Headland Archaeology Ltd for supporting us in writing this paper, particularly Damian Shiels and Jean Price for editing and commenting on an earlier draft of this paper; to Brendon Wilkins, Liam McKinstry, Tara Doyle and Joanne Hughes for access to the material and results; and to Sara Nylund and Scott Harrison for the graphics.

Notes

1. Kilcloghans: NGR 142990, 253830; height 46 m OD; excavation licence no. 06E1139.
2. Carrowkeel: NGR 159326, 22349; height 45 m OD; excavation reg. no. E2046; ministerial direction no. A024; RMP no. GA097-066.
3. Moyle Big: NGR 277216, 173509; height 200–300 m OD; excavation reg. no. E2598; ministerial direction no. A021.
4. Ballyvass: NGR 276870, 187816; height 96–8 m OD; excavation reg. no. E2996; ministerial direction no. A021.

9. A fixed abode: Neolithic houses in County Carlow

TJ O'Connell and Nial O'Neill

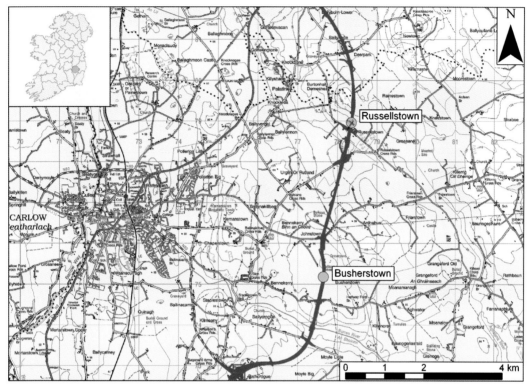

Illus. 1—Location of the sites at Russellstown and Busherstown, Co. Carlow (based on the Ordnance Survey Ireland map).

The type of evidence that archaeologists uncover for Neolithic settlement in Ireland can come in a variety of forms, ranging from small-scale temporary sites to larger, more permanent enclosed landscapes such as the Céide fields in County Mayo. Neolithic buildings form one part of this mosaic of settlement evidence. The remains of two Early Neolithic rectangular houses were excavated in the townlands of Russellstown and Busherstown, Co. Carlow, by Headland Archaeology Ltd in 2006 on behalf of Carlow County Council and the NRA.[1] This work was undertaken in advance of construction works for the N9/N10 Kilcullen–Waterford Road Scheme: Prumpelstown to Powerstown (Illus. 1). Their identification and excavation provide important additions to our knowledge of this site type in a part of the country where they have not been documented previously. Prior to the discovery of these buildings, evidence of Neolithic settlement in County Carlow was limited to a number of impressive funerary monuments, such as Kernanstown Portal Tomb (Record of Monuments and Places no. CW007-010), known locally as Brownshill Dolmen, and the Baunogenasraid Linkardstown-type burial tomb (CW008-031001). Both the Russellstown and Busherstown sites were located within a 3.5 km radius of Brownshill Dolmen and within 5 km of the Baunogenasraid tumulus. Although it cannot be proven at present, the likelihood that those involved in building these tombs may have lived in one or both of the houses under discussion cannot be discounted.

Early Neolithic buildings are being uncovered in increasing numbers throughout Ireland. A review of the literature concerning these structures shows that they often share a number of elements in common: for example, a marked preference for upland sitings on south- or south-west-facing slopes in areas of good soils, with access to a water source (Cooney & Grogan 1999, 42–7). The ground-plans of these buildings also share a number of common characteristics: most are defined by a substantial rectangular or square foundation trench, with the greatest number aligned north-east–south-west, east–west or north-west–south-east. Various building sizes have been recorded, with a tight cluster measuring 6–8 m long by 4–7 m wide (Smyth 2006, 234). A significant number of houses were constructed using a combination of posts, planks and wattle walling (ibid., 238). Internal division sometimes occurred, with one, two or three rooms or compartments within one structure (Grogan 2004, 107). In addition to the walls, internal arrangements of post-holes would have provided support for the roof, which was likely to have been made of thatch (Cooney 2000, 58–9). Evidence for a hearth or the remains of a hearth sometimes occurs (Smyth 2006, 241). Doorways are rarely identified; those that have been recorded, however, generally occur on the gable end walls or at the corners of the buildings (Grogan 2004, 107). Although there is a general consensus in Ireland that these buildings were domestic in nature, some question the role of Early Neolithic buildings as dwelling-places and suggest alternative functions for them, for example as meeting places or cult houses where activities such as feasting occurred (Topping 1996; Cooney 2003, 52). Finally, in over half the examples of excavated Early Neolithic buildings, substantial burning of the structure has taken place (Smyth 2006, 246).

Russellstown

The first building under discussion was excavated in Russellstown, on the south-west-facing slope of a small hill capped by the walled, 18th-century demesne of Burtonhall, approximately 5 km north-east of Carlow town. Stream channels were located c. 300 m to the south-west of the site near the lower slopes of the hill.

The excavation was directed by Linda Hegarty and was carried out in February–April 2006. A total area of almost 15,000 m² was stripped of topsoil, revealing a variety of archaeological features cut into the underlying subsoil (Illus. 2). In addition to the Early Neolithic phase, the site was reused during the Final Neolithic/Early Bronze Age period, the Bronze Age and again later in the medieval period. Initially, it had been thought that the Early Neolithic building was enclosed by a large curvilinear ditch partly exposed within the road corridor (Logan 2007). A radiocarbon date of AD 903–1038 (UBA-8730; see Appendix 1 for details) was, however, returned for some charred barley grains from the upper ditch fills, providing a medieval date for the infilling of the upper portion of this feature.

The remains of the Early Neolithic building were located on a flat ridge on the slope of the hill. They were initially revealed as charcoal-enriched soil that formed a subrectangular shape, aligned NNE–SSW, that continued to the east beyond the area of excavation. Excavation revealed that the remains represented structural material within a

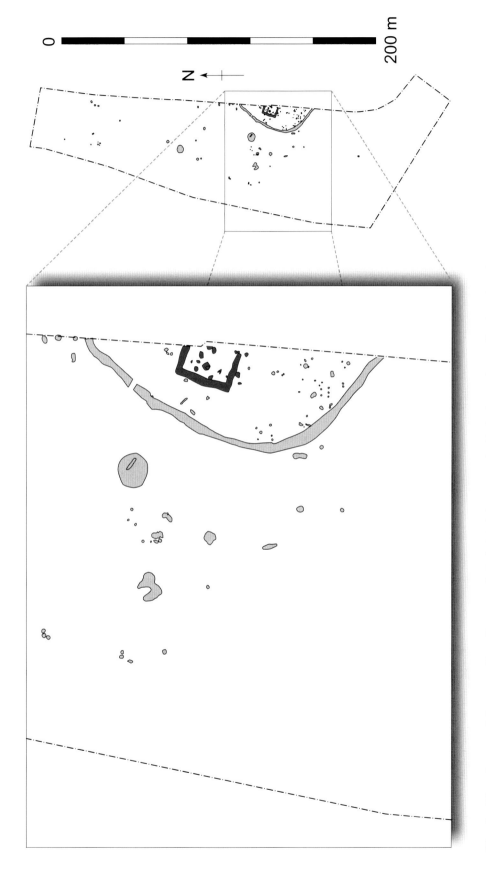

Illus. 2—Plan of excavated features at Russellstown, with Early Neolithic activity highlighted in red (Headland Archaeology Ltd).

0

200 m

N

continuous subrectangular foundation trench. A possible entranceway was identified on the south-east side, where the southern foundation trench terminated near the edge of the road corridor. Internal features included a post-pit, a post-hole, pits and a possible hearth (Illus. 3 & 4).

The portion of the foundation trench within the area of excavation measured 8.5 m by 6 m. It was U-shaped in profile but the width and depth varied between the three excavated sides. The western portion was 0.55–0.6 m wide and 0.3–0.48 m deep. The northern portion was only exposed for 3.5 m and measured 0.7–0.9 m in width and 0.6–0.9 m in depth. The southern portion was the least substantial, 0.32–0.38 m wide and 0.15–0.35 m deep. This portion terminated near the eastern edge of the site, suggesting the location of a possible entranceway. The remains of three possible post-holes and one burnt post (partly within the excavation area) were evident within the foundation trench. These were set into and partly truncated its base. Their presence was only revealed after the excavation of the foundation trench packing fill.

The burnt, and likely in parts decayed, remains of a plank wall were located within the foundation trench. This wall appeared to have been continuous originally, but the evidence of its presence varied along the course of the trench. For example, within the western portion its presence was indicated by charcoal-rich soil, while in the northern and southern portions its course was less well defined. The timber planks were shown in section to have had vertical sides and a flat base. Their recorded depth within the trench was 0.2–0.45 m. Surrounding the remains of the plank wall and filling the foundation trench was a packing fill that incorporated approximately 30 stones to support the wall. The majority of these were subrounded granite cobbles with an average diameter of 0.3 m. Charred hazelnut shells that were recovered from the remains of the plank wall and the surrounding packing fill underwent radiocarbon dating and returned date ranges of 3707–3636 BC (UBA-8731) and 3776–3657 BC (UBA-8734), dating the building to the Early Neolithic period.

A post-pit and a post-hole within the building formed a linear alignment with a possible post-hole in the western portion of the foundation trench. This line of posts, running down the middle of the building, could have supported the apex of the roof and suggests a possible internal division within the building. A number of shallow pits were located within the structure. Their function was unclear but they may have served as rubbish pits for domestic waste. A patch of oxidised clay subsoil, measuring 1 m east–west by 0.7 m north–south, was located 3.2 m from the northern foundation trench and appeared to denote the location of a possible hearth. A post-hole and two pits were situated outside the southern end of the building. The post-hole is likely to have provided additional support for the wall. Charred hazelnut shells recovered from one of the pits suggested that they were used for the disposal of domestic waste (Stewart 2008a).

The artefacts recovered from the building included a range of stone tools, pottery (Illus. 5 & 6) and small fragments of burnt bone (unidentifiable to species), and suggest a domestic function for the structure. They included a flint concave scraper, a granite hammerstone and numerous sherds of Early Neolithic Carinated Bowl pottery (round-bottomed vessels with distinct shoulders, or carinations, generally having curved necks). Possible evidence for the gathering of foodstuffs and the cultivation of cereals was recovered from the fills of the foundation trenches and associated features. This included carbonised hazelnut shells and grains of emmer wheat, one of the first grains to be cultivated in Ireland (ibid.). It is also possible, however, that the shells derive from the gathering of firewood.

Illus. 3—The Early Neolithic house remains at Russellstown (Headland Archaeology Ltd).

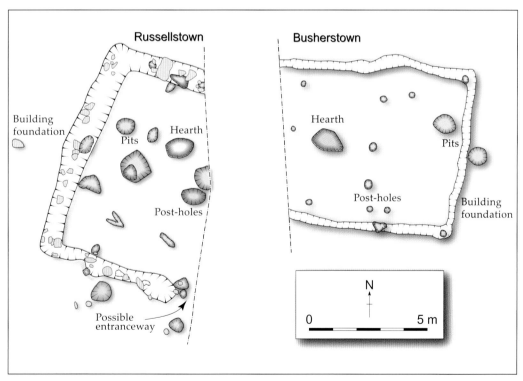

Illus. 4—Ground-plans of the two Early Neolithic houses (Headland Archaeology Ltd).

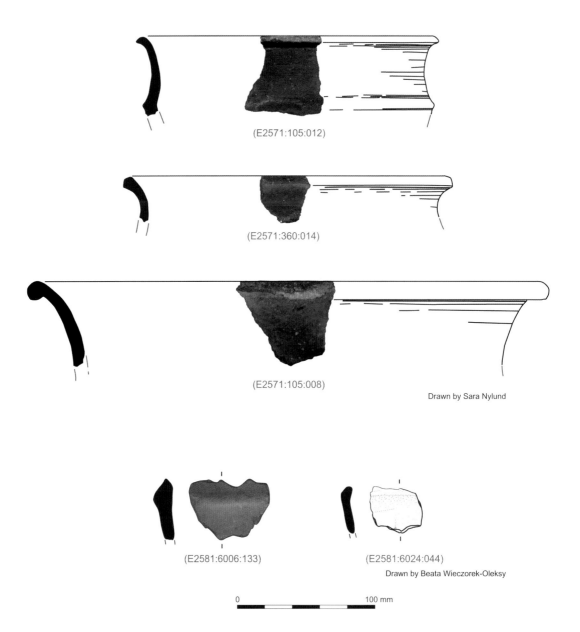

(E2571:105:012)

(E2571:360:014)

(E2571:105:008)

Drawn by Sara Nylund

(E2581:6006:133)

(E2581:6024:044)

Drawn by Beata Wieczorek-Oleksy

0   100 mm

Illus. 5—Early Neolithic Carinated Bowl sherds from Russellstown (top three) and Busherstown (bottom two) (Headland Archaeology Ltd).

Other examples of Early Neolithic buildings have been shown to have been destroyed by fire, and this may also have happened at Russellstown. The packing fills surrounding the burnt post and plank remains within the foundation trench were heavily oxidised, indicating that the walls and post were burnt *in situ*. The reason for this type of destruction is not clear: it may have been accidental or it may have been a deliberate act.

Busherstown

At Busherstown, 4.5 km east of Carlow town and 4 km south of Russellstown, the remains of a foundation trench were uncovered on the lower part of a south-facing gentle slope,

Illus. 6—Stone tools from Russellstown: (top) possible concave scraper, disc scraper and naturally backed knife (all flint); (bottom) rubbing stone and hammer/rubbing stone (Headland Archaeology Ltd).

next to the western limit of the excavation area (Illus. 7). The River Burren is less than 1 km to the south, with a tributary 300 m to the east.

The foundation trench was located next to the western edge of the road corridor, with the trench continuing beyond it. The remains within the limit of excavation were rectangular in plan, aligned east–west, 8.4 m long and 6.4 m wide (Illus. 4 & 8). Upon excavation it became apparent that the trench represented the remains of an Early Neolithic structure owing to the recovery of numerous sherds of Early Neolithic Carinated Bowl pottery (Illus. 5) (MacSween 2008) within its fill. A probable hearth was recorded towards the western portion of the excavated area, with several post- and stake-holes appearing to denote internal divisions.

Almost 22 m of continuous foundation trench was excavated, and three post-holes were recorded at the base of the trench. The trench had a U-shaped profile and was 0.45 m in width and 0.3 in depth. One of the post-holes was located at the north-eastern corner, with the second at the south-eastern corner and the third 2.5 m west of the south-eastern corner along the southern portion of the wall. These post-holes were cut c. 0.2 m in depth below the base of the trench and appeared to be the support posts for a wattle and daub wall. Also contained within the fill of the trench was one piece of struck flint, frequent charcoal and

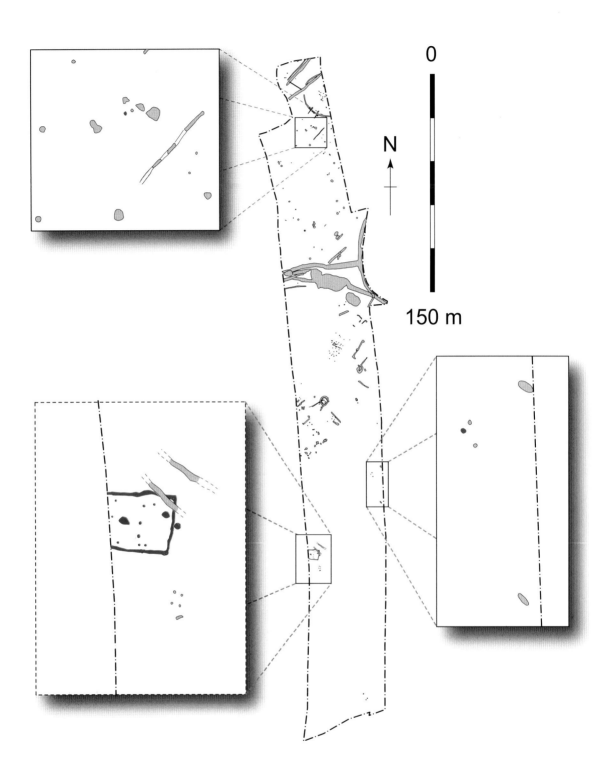

Illus. 7—Site plan of excavated features at Busherstown, with Early Neolithic activity highlighted in red (Headland Archaeology Ltd).

Illus. 8—Excavation of the Early Neolithic house remains at Busherstown (Headland Archaeology Ltd).

fire-reddened clay. The trench was 0.3 m in depth and would not have been deep enough to support a plank wall such as that uncovered at Russellstown. There was no evidence that the trench had been truncated by ploughing or in any other way denuded, for example by soil erosion. In addition, it was notable that the fill of the trench did not contain packing stones, which would have been vital in helping to support a plank wall.

An oxidised area of subsoil has been interpreted as evidence of a probable hearth towards the western end of the structure, but it was the eastern end that attracted most attention. Here a line of post-holes running north–south, perpendicular to the alignment of the structure, appeared to internally divide off 3.5 m of the length of the structure. What was most surprising was a pit located within this area that contained sherds of Early Neolithic Carinated Bowl pottery, both stratigraphically above and at the same level as a deposit containing unidentifiable burnt bone within a charcoal-rich fill. This feature appeared to have all the hallmarks of a Bronze Age cremation pit yet contained Early Neolithic pottery. A radiocarbon date obtained from the bone indicates that it dates from the period 3517–3358 BC (UBA-8447). This date range straddles the later part of the Early Neolithic and the early Middle Neolithic period, and the presence of Neolithic Carinated Bowl pottery in both the foundation trench and the pit appears to suggest that the pottery in the pit may be residual.

A second line of three internal post-holes was located 2.5–3.5 m further west of the line discussed above. These post-holes were also roughly aligned north–south. Inside the area demarcated by these two lines of post-holes was the probable hearth.

A large post-hole or possible pit was located immediately outside the structure to the east. This feature truncated a smaller post-hole and may have been a support post for the wall.

A small pit c. 65 m north-east of the structure was found to contain a large struck flint in the form of a convex end scraper of Late Mesolithic/Early Neolithic date (Sternke 2008, 9). A second small pit 350 m north of the foundation trench was also found to contain Neolithic Carinated Bowl pottery.

Charred hazelnut shells were recovered from the site, along with cereal grains that were, unfortunately, too degraded to allow for species identification. Nevertheless, the presence of such grains along with hazelnut shells and a hearth suggests a domestic function for this structure.

As with the house at Russellstown, the presence of fire-reddened clay in the foundation trench suggests that the house may have met its end through fire.

Discussion

Both structures appear to conform to the characteristics that have become accepted as typical of an Early Neolithic house. The presence of a hearth, internal divisions, cereal grains, hazelnut shells and pottery all indicate that these structures likely fulfilled a domestic function.

The layout of both houses was remarkably similar to previously published examples, such as Ballyglass, Co. Mayo (Ó Nualláin 1972), Corbally 1, Co. Kildare (Purcell 2002), and Newtown, Co. Meath (Gowen & Halpin 1992). Despite some variation, the rectangular shape or outline of a continuous foundation trench with internal division(s) characterised these sites. Whereas the example at Russellstown was aligned north-east–south-west, the structure at Busherstown was aligned east–west, and these orientations have been shown to be the most common for this monument type (Smyth 2006, 237).

Grogan (2004) has described the 'plank-built' method as the most common construction method, and the house at Russellstown was clearly built using this technique. More recent evidence, however, indicates that a significant number of houses were built using the 'wattle-and-daub' technique, sometimes in combination with planks. The house at Busherstown appears to have been an example of this type.

Carbonised hazelnut shells and grains of emmer wheat, one of the first cereals to be cultivated in Ireland, were found on the Russellstown site, and charred hazelnut shells and cereal grain too degraded for species identification were found at Busherstown (Stewart 2008b). Hazelnut shells have been found on the majority of similar sites across the country, while cereal grain has been recovered from many sites, including Corbally 1, 2 and 3 (Purcell 2002), Tankardstown, Co. Limerick (Gowen & Tarbett 1988), and Ballyglass (Ó Nualláin 1972), among others.

It is becoming increasingly apparent that this monument type dates from the earlier part of the Neolithic period. In a recent article McSparron (2008) found that through careful selection of reliable radiocarbon dates for this monument type a clearly defined date range from 3715 to 3625 BC was obtained at a 95.4% confidence level. The radiocarbon date returned for the Russellstown house falls neatly into this date range, while Neolithic Carinated Bowl pottery is also understood to date from this period (Gibson 2002, 69–74). Although a reliable radiocarbon date could not be obtained for the house at Busherstown, the presence of typologically distinct Carinated Bowl pottery suggests that the structure was also from this period. Furthermore, the burnt bone in the pit containing Carinated Bowl

Illus. 9—Reconstruction of the house at Russellstown (drawn by Sara Nylund, Headland Archaeology Ltd).

pottery within the Busherstown structure was dated to just after the period outlined by McSparron (2008) and, presuming that human or animal remains were not interred within an occupied house, may indicate the final use/abandonment of this structure. The date (3517–3358 BC) obtained from the bone could suggest that this pottery type continued in use in south-east Ireland beyond the first centuries of the Neolithic period. It has been commonly accepted that Carinated Bowl pottery was being made in Ireland from 4000 to 3600 BC, and probably continued to be made after this date (Sheridan 1995, 17; Gibson 2002, 70). It remains highly probable, however, that this pottery was residual and may have been placed in the pit, along with the burnt bone, after the abandonment of the house.

Destruction through fire is possible, given the presence of fire-reddened clay in the foundation trenches of both structures. There is a growing corpus of evidence that deliberate destruction of Early Neolithic houses occurred relatively frequently. It has also been postulated that this destruction may have been part of the perceived 'life cycle' of these houses (Bailey 1996). Experiments carried out by Bankoff and Winter (1979) showed that the complete destruction of an Early Neolithic house was a calculated act and involved sustained effort over many hours. A particularly conspicuous example was recently uncovered during archaeological works in advance of the N2 Carrickmacross Bypass at Monanny, Co. Monaghan (Walsh 2006). Here completely burnt and charred posts were uncovered among the structural remains within 'House C'; this appeared to be clear evidence for the deliberate burning of that structure. While such pronounced evidence was

Illus. 10—Reconstruction of the house at Busherstown (drawn by Eavan O'Dochartaigh, Headland Archaeology Ltd).

not uncovered at Busherstown or Russellstown, fire-reddened clay was observed in the foundation trenches of both houses. Bankoff and Winter's (1979) experiment demonstrated that the burning of subsurface structural remains only occurred through sustained effort, and so it remains highly probable that these two examples also 'died' through fire.

Conclusion

While the remains of both houses partly extended beyond the road corridor, a significant portion of each was situated within the areas of excavation, enough to determine the layout and form of the houses (Illus. 9 & 10). Their shape, orientation and the layout of internal features were all within the established parameters for such structures, and both methods of wall construction clearly belonged to the architectural tradition of the period. The range of finds, including stone tools and pottery, were all typically Neolithic. The type of material culture and environmental material recovered suggests a domestic function for the buildings, offering us a glimpse into the everyday lives of their inhabitants. This provides a tangible connection to Carlow's Neolithic tomb-builders and ties the two structures to the wider landscape.

Acknowledgements

We would like to thank NRA Archaeologist Noel Dunne, Senior Archaeologist Colm Moloney, Site Directors Angus Stephenson and Linda Hegarty, and fellow Supervisors Kevin Murphy and Caoimhe Ní Thóibín. We are grateful to Jonathan Millar and all the graphics team for their illustration work, to Carmelita Troy and Susan Lalonde for analysis of the cremated bone, to Karen Stewart for palaeoenvironmental analysis, and to Jean Price for commenting on drafts of this paper. Special thanks go to the staff and the excavation crews of Headland Archaeology Ltd for their hard work and dedication, without which none of this would have been possible.

Note

1. Russellstown: NGR 278344, 178957; height 83 m OD; excavation reg. no. E2571; ministerial direction no. A021; excavation director Linda Hegarty.
Busherstown: NGR 277758, 175185; height 88 m OD; excavation reg. no. E2581; ministerial direction no. A021; excavation director Angus Stephenson.

10. No corners! Prehistoric roundhouses on the N8 and N7 in counties Cork, Tipperary and Offaly

John Tierney and Penny Johnston

During excavation, interpretative theories abound among members of the excavation team on the site. These are reviewed and tested in the post-excavation phase and reviewed again as more excavations take place and new evidence comes to light. In recent years, Eachtra Archaeological Projects has excavated a range of prehistoric structures in varying states of preservation and of varying complexity. One of the most common types is the circular house or roundhouse, usually dated to the Bronze Age. This paper presents a developing understanding of the patterns evident in the archaeological remains of roundhouses, an understanding that is changing as our ability to analyse detail and measurements quickly is being transformed by the fact that we have started to record our excavations directly into a Geographical Information Systems (GIS) package. This package combines a map of the site with a database of the archaeology found, allowing the various aspects of an archaeological site (context of recovery, soil samples and artefacts) to be viewed as a whole. This technology, along with an increased ability to produce 3D models of excavated structures, has breathed new life into the way we approach and interpret the buildings of the past.

The projects

The evidence that we examine here is of prehistoric structures found during some excavations along the routes of new roads in Cork, Tipperary and Offaly (Illus. 1 & 2). In County Cork, excavations of five roundhouses were carried out in advance of construction along the routes of the N8 Mitchelstown Relief Road in 2005 and the N8 Fermoy–Mitchelstown road scheme in 2006–7, with sites at Mitchelstown 1, structures A, B and C (Illus. 3), Kilshanny 1 and Ballynamona 2 (Illus. 4).[1] These sites were excavated on behalf of Cork County Council and the NRA.

In Tipperary and Offaly, eight roundhouses, or partial round structures, were excavated along the route of the N7 Castletown–Nenagh: Derrinsallagh to Ballintottty road scheme in 2007–8, at sites at Drumbaun 2, Co. Tipperary, structures A and B (Illus. 5), Drumroe 1, Co. Offaly (Illus. 6), Castleroan 1, Co. Offaly, structures A and B, Moatquarter, Co. Tipperary, and Derrybane 2, Co. Tipperary, structures 1 and 2.[2] These sites were excavated on behalf of Laois County Council and the NRA.

Only the structures from Mitchelstown 1, excavated in 2005, currently have radiocarbon dates. All three structures from this site were dated to the Middle Bronze Age; material from structure A returned a radiocarbon date of 1493–1305 BC (UB-6771; see Appendix 1 for details), structure B was dated to 1431–1267 BC (UB-6774) and structure C was dated to 1419–1213 BC (UB-6773). The post-excavation work on the remaining excavations is still ongoing but radiocarbon results are anticipated soon. Therefore the remaining buildings are tentatively assigned to the Bronze Age based on typology, with the understanding that this classification may have to be revised in the near future.

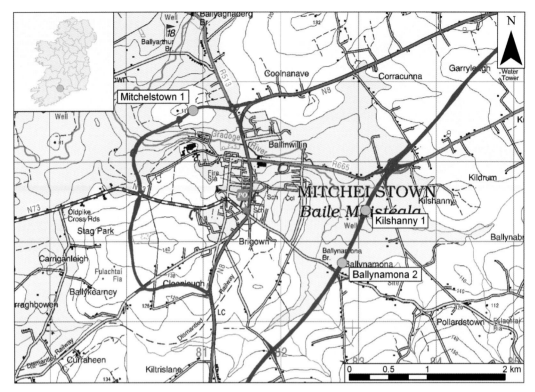

Illus. 1—Location of sites in County Cork discussed in this paper (based on the Ordnance Survey Ireland map).

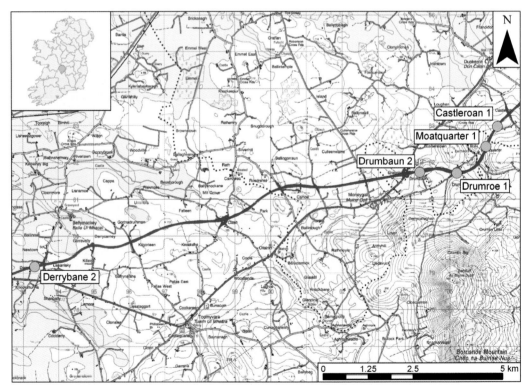

Illus. 2—Location of sites in counties Tipperary and Offaly discussed in this paper (based on the Ordnance Survey Ireland map).

Illus. 3—Elevated view of roundhouses A, B and C excavated at Mitchelstown 1, Co. Cork, from north-east. The dashed lines only show the main structural elements of each structure and not the hypothesised wall lines differentiated from the drip-gully of structure A (Eachtra Archaeological Projects).

Illus. 4 (below)— Excavations at Ballynamona 2 roundhouse, Co. Cork, from the south-west (John Sunderland).

Illus. 5—Excavations of structure A at Drumbaun 2, Co. Tipperary, from the east (John Sunderland).

Reconstructing the past: 3D models of Bronze Age houses

Reconstruction modelling is an area of growing technological development. In order to recreate accurately a likeness of a prehistoric building, archaeologists must engage with issues such as the nature of walls, their location, identification of the main structural supports, baseplates, wall-plates, rafters, roofing materials, thatching styles, etc. It goes beyond a simple record of layout and dimensions. This is sometimes quite difficult, particularly since most Irish prehistoric roundhouses have no surviving superstructure (Doody 2007, 92). The exercise of 3D modelling, however, forces us to nail our colours to the mast.

Some of our decisions are based on evidence that has been collated from a number of different excavations of Bronze Age houses. The size and type of the structure influence the type of material that is used in the superstructure. The relatively large scale of our roundhouses and the evidence for substantial support posts suggest that the roof was quite heavy, possibly made from thatch. A combination of lighter wattling may have been interspersed between heavier timbers: examples of hazel and willow wattling are known from Ballyveelish 3, Co. Tipperary (Doody 1987), and Knockadoon at Lough Gur, Co. Limerick (Cleary 1995). There is generally very little evidence for wall coverings, however. Daub was found at Grange and Ballingoola, Co. Limerick, and at Lisheen and Curraghatoor, Co. Tipperary (Doody 2007, 93). Some walls may also have been covered in animal skins, and several houses may have had walls partly made from sods. A generic idea of what Bronze Age roundhouses may have looked like is presented in Illus. 7, a computer-

Illus. 6—Entrance to the roundhouse excavated at Drumroe 1, Co. Offaly, from east (Eachtra Archaeological Projects).

Illus. 7—Reconstruction of two roundhouses at Mitchelstown 1 (Digitale Archäologie).

generated reconstruction of structures A and B excavated at Mitchelstown 1, Co. Cork. This illustration is a still from a 3D-animated representation of the site created by Digitale Archäologie, which has featured in an exhibition in Cork Public Museum (Conran 2008; Hanley 2008). In this reconstruction both structures appear very alike. A re-evaluation of the Mitchelstown house plans was called for, however, in the light of new discoveries and more recent excavations.

Comparing Mitchelstown 1 to local examples of Bronze Age houses was relatively easy in north Cork as two houses, possibly of similar date to Mitchelstown (pending radiocarbon dates), were excavated at Kilshanny 1 and Ballynamona 2.

At both Kilshanny 1 and Ballynamona 2 the narrow foundation trenches of the houses were associated with post-holes, but the post-holes did not form an arc and there was no obvious pattern to their arrangement. The perimeter of Kilshanny 1 was 61.7 m in length and the perimeter of Ballynamona 2 (structure A) was 56.05 m. This is larger than some post-built roundhouses; for example, the perimeter of the ring of posts in structure A at Mitchelstown 1 was 23.4 m. Even when the perimeter of Mitchelstown 1 is measured to include the linear trench (which does not survive all the way around the house) it is much smaller, at 31 m, than the perimeters of Ballynamona 2 and Kilshanny 1.

This begs the question as to the function of the curvilinear trenches around the circular houses. At Ballynamona 2 the trench was extremely narrow (0.18 m wide and between 0.12 m and 0.18 m deep) and did not include support posts. This was too insubstantial to form the foundation of the building, and much of the support for the roof probably came from internal post-holes. The excavator, Linda Hegarty, noted impressions of straight panels visible at regular intervals (each panel c. 1 m in length) along the top of the trench, and speculated that the trench housed upright panels of wattle-and-daub or planks that formed non-load-bearing walls around the house. The excavator of Mitchelstown 1, Eamonn Cotter, also interpreted the curvilinear trench around structure A as a wall, although the trench was not as well defined as the example at Ballynamona 2 or at Kilshanny 1. On the other hand, some interpret the irregular trenches around the structures as drip-gullies, channelling water that ran off from the roof. If some of the trenches were drip-gullies, their identification as such provides evidence for the extent of the overhang of the roof. All these considerations affect the way that we then reconstruct these buildings.

For example, does the fact that more post-holes were found near the back of a structure suggest that the roof needed more support in this part of the building? What could cause this? An additional floor or loft at this part of the house, perhaps? Or did the trenches outside the houses serve as additional support for the roof, given that they are generally found near the entrance of houses rather than at the backs, which meant that fewer posts were needed at the front? Or perhaps the deeper and often larger entrance posts at the front of the house meant that not as many post-holes were required in this part of the house. To what extent did the thatched roof overhang the walls? And so on.

These are all ideas to consider, accept or reject. For example, the drip-gully interpretation at Mitchelstown 1 was rejected by the excavator, who thought that the slope at the site would have meant that it channelled water in the wrong direction (i.e. towards the entrance rather than away from it). This demonstrates that in order to take this analysis further we need to engage more intimately with the basic archaeological record as we analyse measurements, not merely looking at detail in plan, but using the field record as the basis for examining other factors as well, such as the depths of different features across the site and their levels. Because the field record is the basis for all of this analysis, it is essential to record these structural features in detail during excavation. Entire reconstructions could hang on post-pipe dimensions or the recorded angle of insertion, for example, and all of these data can be dealt with by GIS.

Using GIS to identify patterns within Bronze Age roundhouses

Using GIS we have identified an interesting pattern in the plans of some roundhouses, one that may have implications for the way we reconstruct the houses. During 2007 two roundhouses were excavated at Drumbaun 2, Co. Tipperary. Based on their typology, these houses were possibly Bronze Age in date. The supervisor on the site, Paul Rondelez, was fascinated by these buildings and he started examining the measurements between the post-holes in one of the roundhouses (structure A). He soon noticed an interesting symmetry: although circular, the house seemed to be arranged on a sort of 'axis' between the entrance and a post-hole directly opposite it. Two post-holes flank the entrance and the remaining post-holes have a corresponding partner at either side of the axis, apart from the single, unpaired post-hole opposite the entrance (see Illus. 8). The distances between post-holes on either side of the axis are roughly the same. This indicates that although the post-holes were not evenly spaced they were symmetrically arranged.

Continuing Paul's site work, our GIS specialist, Maurizio Toscano, investigated whether the remains of other structures excavated by Eachtra along the route of the N7 Castletown–Nenagh road scheme also displayed axial symmetry. His results (Illus. 9 & 10)

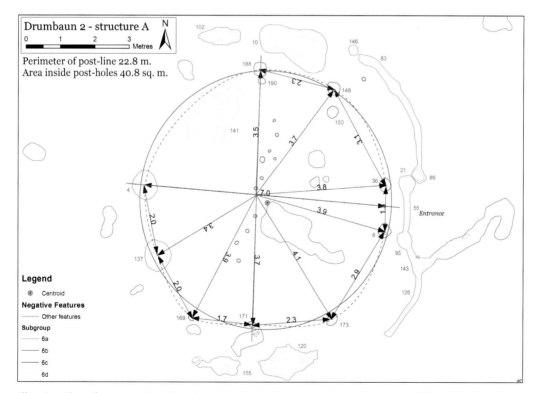

Illus. 8—Plan of structure A at Drumbaun 2, showing the symmetrical arrangement of the post-holes (Eachtra Archaeological Projects).

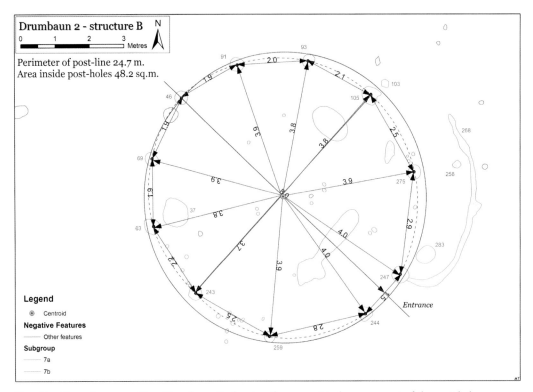

Illus. 9—Plan of structure B at Drumbaun 2, showing the symmetrical arrangement of the post-holes (Eachtra Archaeological Projects).

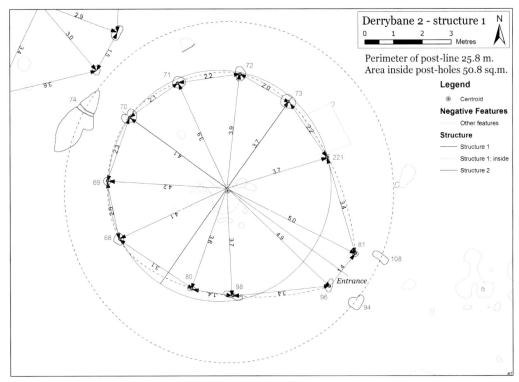

Illus. 10—Plan of structure 1 at Derrybane 2, Co. Tipperary, showing the symmetrical arrangement of the post-holes (Eachtra Archaeological Projects).

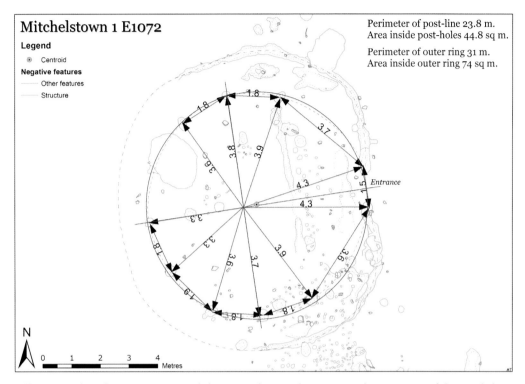

Illus. 11—Plan of structure A at Mitchelstown 1, showing the symmetrical arrangement of the post-holes (Eachtra Archaeological Projects).

demonstrated that at least three of the round, post-built structures were constructed along the same principle (Drumbaun 2, structures A and B, and Derrybane 2, structure 1). The structures at other sites may also originally have been constructed using the same pattern, for example at Castleroan 1, structure B, and at Drumroe 1. Only the partial remains of these buildings were excavated, however, and it is therefore difficult to be certain. On the other hand, some of the excavated prehistoric structures did not fit into this pattern at all. Buildings at Derrybane 2 (structure 2), Castleroan 1 (structure A) and Moatquarter demonstrated no evidence of this symmetrical pattern in their layout. It was therefore a pattern that was identified in three of the eight circular structures excavated as part of the project, and was possibly present in two more structures. This was a relatively large proportion of the structures found during the project. Could this pattern be identified at other sites as well? We applied the same GIS analysis to a wider area, comparing some material gathered from our excavations in north Cork. Of the three post-built roundhouses excavated at Mitchelstown 1, only one building, structure A, demonstrated axial symmetry (Illus. 11).

The analysis also showed that in most of the houses with axial symmetry the post-holes were more closely spaced towards the back of the buildings, rather than near the entrance. In addition, all of the houses demonstrated evidence for trenches near their entrance, with the exception of Derrybane 2, structure 1.

A similar phenomenon has already been identified in roundhouses in Britain. Guilbert (1982, 68–9) identified axial symmetry at Moel y Gaer, Clwyd, Wales, amongst a large number of post-built roundhouses dating from the sixth and fifth centuries BC. These structures were defined by between seven and 13 post-holes, forming a ring 4.3–8 m in diameter, and with an entrance, usually to the south-east, that comprised two to four additional post-holes and resembled entrance porches. Brück's study of 86 Middle Bronze Age roundhouses in southern England also identified 18 buildings (21%) that were constructed using axial symmetry. She suggested that the roundhouses could be seen as a model of the Middle Bronze Age universe in a microcosm (Brück 1999, 155–8). As an interesting aside to this idea, axial symmetry is also evident in the layout of Cork/Kerry-type stone circles, where the entrance is flanked by two portal stones, with an opposing recumbent stone at the other side of the circle, and paired standing stones on either side of the axis between the entrance and the recumbent stone (Ó Nualláin 1984, 3; Fahy 1959, 15).

On a more practical note, does the identification of a clear pattern in the construction of roundhouses add to our understanding of these buildings, how they were built and appeared in the past? Does it mean that structure A at Mitchelstown 1, where the plan of the building demonstrated axial symmetry, looked different to the adjacent structure B, where there was no evidence for axial symmetry? Will this discovery contribute to the way we approach 3D modelling in the future? We hope to move on from our plan-based analysis in the near future to a more thorough 3D GIS analysis of the buildings, to look at issues such as post-hole depth, angles of insertion and levels. This will not merely be for the purposes of reconstruction. It will also enable us to analyse the uniformity and the pattern in the construction of these structures, thereby perhaps identifying more formal patterns in the layout and construction of Irish roundhouses during the Bronze Age.

Acknowledgements

These excavations were overseen by NRA Archaeologists Niall Roycroft and Ken Hanley. Thanks to all the excavation crew for their hard work. Paul Rondelez, Linda Hegarty, Laurence McGowan, James Lyttleton, Rafal Panfil, David O'Reilly and Tomasz Wasowski deserve particular mention, as does Eamonn Cotter, who commented on some early ideas.

Notes

1. Mitchelstown 1: NGR 180869, 113639; height 106 m OD; excavation licence no. 04E1072; excavation director Eamonn Cotter. Kilshanny 1: NGR 183091, 112389; height 95 m OD; excavation reg. no. E2430; ministerial direction no. A040; excavation director James Lyttleton. Ballynamona 2: NGR 182792, 111731; height 95 m OD; excavation reg. no. E2429; ministerial direction no. A040; excavation director Linda Hegarty.
2. Drumbaun 2: NGR 20422, 181746; height 150 m OD; excavation reg. no E3912; ministerial direction no. A038; excavation director John Tierney. Drumroe 1: NGR 205195, 181703; height 160 m OD; excavation reg. no. E3773; ministerial direction no. A038; excavation director John Tierney. Castleroan 1: NGR 206324, 182969; height 160 m OD; excavation reg. no. E3909; ministerial direction no. A038; excavation director John Tierney. Moatquarter: NGR 206009, 182426; height 170 m OD; excavation reg. no. E3910; ministerial direction no. A038; excavation director John Tierney. Derrybane 2: NGR 193326, 179173; height 80 m OD; excavation reg. no. E3591; ministerial direction no. A038; excavation director Laurence McGowan.

11. Hearth and home: Bronze Age structures in south Tipperary

Melanie McQuade and Colm Moriarty

Archaeological investigations in advance of the N8 Cashel–Mitchelstown Road Improvement Scheme identified 57 previously unrecorded sites that ranged in date from the Early Neolithic period (4000–3600 BC) to the post-medieval period (AD 1550–present). The majority of sites (40) produced evidence for Bronze Age activity and this paper focuses on the structural remains from that period.

The road scheme, which opened in July 2008, comprises 41 km of improved dual carriageway from Cashel, Co. Tipperary, to Carrigane, Co. Cork. A link road to the N24 was also constructed to the north-east of Cahir, stretching for 3.8 km between the townlands of Kedrah and Knockmorris (Illus. 1). The road scheme extends south-westwards from Cashel through rolling agricultural lowlands overlooked by the Galty and Knockmealdown mountain ranges further south. Having crossed the River Suir just north of Cahir, the route travels along poorly drained land below the southern break in slope of the Galty Mountains. Here a series of small watercourses run down from the mountains, the largest of which is the River Funshion. The N24 link road runs eastwards from the N8 through an area of elevated farmland, to the north-east of the River Suir.

Following a geophysical survey and a programme of archaeological testing along the route of the road in 2005, excavations were carried out during 2006 and 2007 by Margaret Gowen & Co. Ltd for McCarthy Hyder CarlBro on behalf of South Tipperary County Council and the NRA. Just over half (21) of the excavated Bronze Age sites were settlements. These varied from small scatterings of pits and post-holes to larger sites with several structures. A total of 24 Bronze Age structures were excavated at 17 different sites along the scheme, several of which had evidence for multiple phases of occupation (Illus. 1) (see Appendix 1 for the radiocarbon dating results).

Distribution and siting of settlements

The distribution of settlement sites demonstrates a distinct concentration of activity in the fertile lands around the River Suir within the townlands of Ballylegan, Ballydrehid, Cloghabreedy, Knockgraffon and Killemly, Co. Tipperary. In contrast, there was a noticeable dearth of settlement sites along the 19 km stretch at the southern end of the road scheme, between the townlands of Clonmore North and Carrigane on the south flank of the Galty Mountains, where less-fertile peaty soils occurred (Illus. 1). The identification of hedgerow species from Bronze Age contexts along the northern end of the scheme suggests that some areas had been cleared of tree cover in order to make land available for grazing and/or the cultivation of crops. Little evidence of animal bone survived, but plant remains recovered during excavation indicate that arable farming was practised here (Geber et al. 2009). The availability of water was undoubtedly an important consideration in choosing habitation sites and selecting farmland, and the majority of settlement sites were located within 1 km

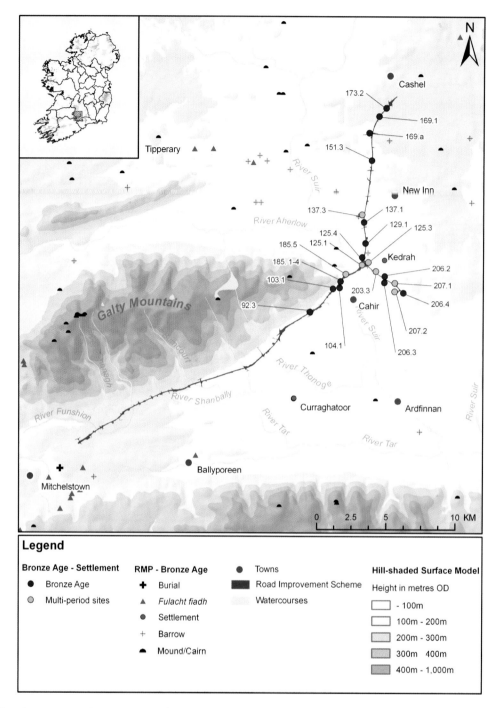

Illus. 1—Location of Bronze Age settlement sites excavated along the route of the N8 Cashel–Mitchelstown Road Improvement Scheme (Margaret Gowen & Co. Ltd).

of a stream or river. The distribution of sites also demonstrates a preference for gradual south- and east-facing slopes, which represent the sunniest and driest locations in the landscape (see Cooney & Grogan 1999) and would also have been relatively sheltered from the prevailing south-westerly winds.

Nature of settlement evidence

The evidence indicates that the Bronze Age population in this part of the country lived in unenclosed settlements. Most of these represented single homesteads but some larger sites with two or more buildings were also recorded.

The earliest Bronze Age settlement evidence came from three Final Neolithic/Early Bronze Age sites, which were dated by finds of Beaker pottery to c. 2500–2200 BC. These sites appeared as scatters of pits and post-holes and are typical of the settlement evidence from this period in Ireland, where a relatively small number of structures are recorded. More substantial evidence was uncovered for the Middle and Late Bronze Age periods, with the majority of settlement sites dating from the Middle Bronze Age (Table 1).

Table 1—Number of Bronze Age settlement sites and structures according to date.

Date	Settlement sites	Structures
Final Neolithic/ Early Bronze Age (also known as Beaker period) (c. 2500–2200 BC)	3	0
Early Bronze Age (c. 2200–1700 BC)	4	1?
Middle Bronze Age (c. 1700–1100 BC)	24	16
Late Bronze Age (c. 1100–600 BC)	9	7

Several sites demonstrated a continuity of settlement during the Bronze Age. At Ballydrehid (site 185.5), for example, radiocarbon dating and artefactual evidence indicated occupation in the Final Neolithic/Early Bronze Age, Middle Bronze Age and Late Bronze Age.[1] At Knockgraffon (site 137.3) a similar prolonged, if episodic, use of the site was evident, with Early, Middle and Late Bronze Age activity being identified.[2] Other sites with evidence for multi-phase activity include Ballylegan (sites 207.1 & 207.2), Cloghabreedy (sites 125.1 & 125.3) and Killemly (site 203.3) (Illus. 1).[3]

Structural design

The structural remains recorded along the road scheme generally represent circular or subcircular buildings, the majority of which measured between 5 m and 7 m in diameter, with some larger examples measuring up to 8.5 m. They compare well with other published examples of Bronze Age roundhouses in Ireland, which typically range from 5 m to 9 m in diameter (Doody 2000, 139; Tierney & Johnston, this volume). Not all of the buildings excavated along the scheme were circular in plan, however. There were subrectangular

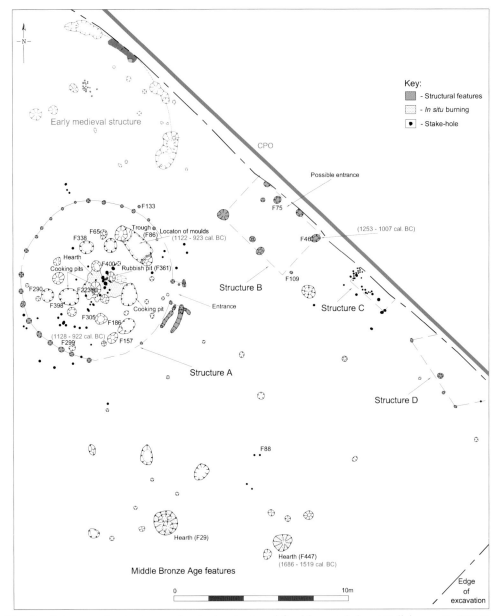

Illus. 2—*Subrectangular structures and a circular structure defined by post-holes at Ballylegan, site 207.2* (Margaret Gowen & Co. Ltd).

structures at Ballylegan (site 207.2) (Illus. 2) and Ballydrehid (structure B, site 185.5) (Illus. 3), a four-posted structure at Knockgraffon (site 137.3) and a D-shaped building at Loughfeedora (site 173.2).[4]

The walls of the structures were defined by post-holes (structure A, Illus. 2), slot-trenches (Illus. 4) or a combination of both (Table 2). The analysis of charcoal remains recovered from these features suggests that the buildings were constructed of oak posts and hazel wattle (Geber et al. 2009). Some of the larger slot-trenches, such as those at Ballydrehid, site 185.5 (Illus. 3), could have supported wooden planks, while alternative walling materials may also have been used, such as earthen sods or even animal skins. The walls may have

Table 2—Types of structures identified along the N8 Cashel–Mitchelstown road scheme.

Ground-plan	Location
Single circle of post-holes	Knockgraffon (sites 137.1 and 137.3), Cloghabreedy (site 125.1), structure A at Ballylegan (site 207.2) (Illus. 2) and Clonmore North (site 92.3)[5]
Circular slot-trench and a concentric ring of internal posts	Structure A at Cloghabreedy (site 125.4) (Illus. 5)[6]
Circular slot-trench foundations	Structure A at Ballydrehid (site 185.5) (Illus. 3) and Ballylegan (site 207.1) (Illus. 4)
Large subrectangular slot-trench foundations	Structure B at Ballydrehid (site 185.5) (Illus. 3)
Subrectangular arrangement of posts	Structures B–D at Ballylegan (site 207.2) (Illus. 2) and Knockgraffon (site 137.3)
Double circuit of post-holes	Structure D at Cloghabreedy (site 125.4) (Illus. 5)
D-shaped arrangement of posts	Loughfeedora (site 173.2)

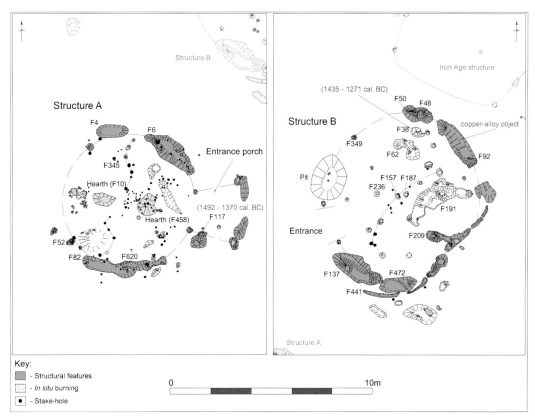

Illus. 3—Circular structure (structure A) and subrectangular structure (structure B) with slot-trench foundations at Ballydrehid, site 185.5 (Margaret Gowen & Co. Ltd).

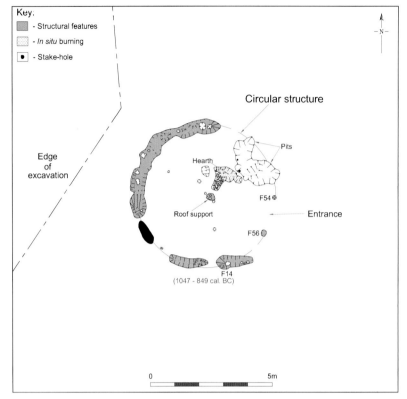

Illus. 4—Slot-trenches defining circular structure, with central roof support, at Ballylegan, site 207.1 (Margaret Gowen & Co. Ltd).

been weatherproofed by the addition of mud daub, burnt fragments of which were recovered from structure A at Ballydrehid, site 185.5. The use of daub has been recorded from other Bronze Age sites such as Grange and Ballingoola, Co. Limerick, as well as Lisheen and Curraghtoor, Co. Tipperary (Doody 2007, 93).

The circular buildings probably had conical roofs of thatch or sod (Illus. 6). The roof would have rested on the external wall, possibly with an inner circuit of roof supports (Cloghabreedy structures A and D; Illus. 5) or a centrally placed post (Illus. 4). Some structures, such as Knockgraffon (site 137.1) and Cloghabreedy (site 125.1), had no internal post-holes, which may indicate that their roofs were supported entirely by the external walls. Experimental reconstructions have shown that thatched conical roofs do not require internal supports, provided that a correct roof angle of 45° is maintained (http://www.flagfen.com/iron_age_roundhouse.htm, accessed November 2008). This angle also allows rainwater to be shed quickly and efficiently.

A second possibility is that the ring of posts that defined several structures, such as Ballylegan (site 207.2; Illus. 2), may be the remains of roof supports rather than the external wall, in which case the external non-load-bearing walls could have been made of lightweight material such as sods or wattle that may not have left an archaeological impression (see Drewett 1982, 327; Cleary 1995). The building remains indicate that wood and/or other organic materials were predominantly used for construction and it is likely that these would have required regular maintenance and repair, evidence of which was recorded at several of the structures.

Entrances were evident at just over half of the 24 structures, and they varied from simple gaps between post-holes (Ballylegan, site 207.1; Illus. 4) to more substantial porches

114

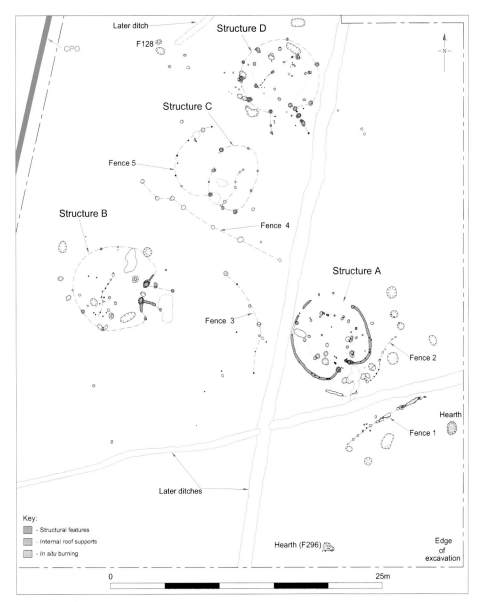

Illus. 5—Structural remains and sections of fencing at Cloghabreedy, site 125.4 (Margaret Gowen & Co. Ltd).

(Cloghabreedy, structures B & D, site 125.4; Illus. 5; Ballydrehid, structure A; Illus. 3) that would have afforded greater protection from the elements; the average door width was 0.8 m. Entrances tended to face the south-east or east, thus avoiding the prevailing south-westerly winds while also maximising the amount of natural light entering the buildings. A smaller number of north-west-, north-, south-west- and west-facing doorways were also recorded, however. In some instances these were in buildings that appeared to have had a non-domestic function, while in clustered settlements such as Cloghabreedy (site 125.4) the entrances of some buildings (structure B) were orientated towards what was presumably the main residence (structure A) (Illus. 5).

Illus. 6—Reconstruction of a Late Bronze Age house excavated at Knockgraffon, site 137.3 (Johnny Ryan for Margaret Gowen & Co. Ltd).

Use of internal space and the function of the buildings

Having described their design and construction methods, discussion now moves to the use of internal space and the function of the structures. Internal divisions, defined by short lines of post-holes or stake-holes, were evident within several buildings. In each case these divisions appeared to separate the rear of the building from the front (Illus. 2 & 4). Assuming that light entered mainly through the doorways at the front of the building, these internal divisions would have left the back of the structure largely in darkness. This area may have been used for sleeping in, while the brighter front of the building may have been more suited to daytime activities such as food preparation. Similar divisions, separating the front of the building from the rear, have been recorded at Bronze Age structures elsewhere in Ireland, for example at Caltragh, Co. Sligo, Tober, Co. Offaly, and Knockdomny, Co. Westmeath (Danaher 2007; Walsh 2007; Hull 2007, 348).

No intact floor levels survived in any of the excavated structures, and only six of the buildings had evidence for internal hearths. External hearths were recorded in several instances, indicating that some buildings may not have had an internal fireplace and, if such buildings had served as dwellings, their occupants may have done their cooking outdoors. It is possible that some of the buildings could have had a raised hearth, which would have left little or no archaeological evidence. Alternatively, the absence of internal hearths and floor levels may be due to truncation caused by deep ploughing, which had left furrows across many of the sites. Whatever the reason for their absence, hearths are not recorded frequently within Bronze Age structures and Doody's (2000, 145) study recorded an incidence of only about 30%. Interestingly, an unusual example of a building with two internal hearths, one in each room, was recorded at structure A in Ballydrehid (site 185.5) (Illus. 3).

Pits were frequently recorded within structures, which is not surprising since they have a greater chance of surviving truncation than other non-cut features. Internal pits appear to

Illus. 7—Decorated spindle-whorl from Killemly, site 203.3 (John Sunderland).

Illus. 8—Baked clay loom-weight (99 mm long) from Knockgraffon, site 137.1 (John Sunderland).

have been used for refuse disposal or storage purposes. The analysis of charred plant remains recovered from such pits indicates that the diet of the occupants comprised cultivated crops (barley and wheat) as well as wild foods (hazelnuts, cherries, crab-apples). One of the pits within structure A at Knockgraffon (site 137.1) contained large quantities of charred cereal grain, indicating that it may have been used to store harvested crops. Grain storage pits are a common feature of the archaeological record in Britain, where experimental archaeology has shown them to be an efficient way of storing crops (Shaw 2003). Other evidence for the processing of foodstuffs comes from saddle querns, two examples of which were reused as packing stones within the foundation trenches of structure B at Ballydrehid (site 185.5). The recovery of pottery sherds is also an indicator of domestic activity related to the preparation, storage and consumption of food. Visible accretions were noted on several sherds of domestic Cordoned Urn recovered from Cloghabreedy (site 125.4),

Illus. 9—Metalworking mould from Ballylegan, site 207.2 (John Sunderland).

demonstrating that they came from vessels that had been used for food preparation (Grogan & Roche 2009).

While small amounts of food could have been stored and/or processed within dwelling-houses, other buildings may have been constructed specifically for the purpose of storing grain. The four-posted structure at Knockgraffon (site 137.3) and three slightly larger multi-post structures at Ballylegan (Illus. 2) are very similar to raised granaries recorded on Bronze Age sites in Britain, such as those from Hayne Lane, Devon, Green Park, Reading, and Thorny Down, Wiltshire (Fitzpatrick et al. 1999, 99, fig. 48; Brossler et al. 2004, 21, fig. 3.7; Brück 1999, 147, fig. 1). The function of these buildings is difficult to prove, however, since organic plant remains rarely survive in archaeological contexts unless they have been charred, and stored grain is unlikely to have been burnt.

It is also likely that dwellings were multi-purpose buildings where numerous activities besides eating and sleeping were carried out. Many crafts, such as textile production, were probably indoor activities. Evidence of such activities comes from spindle-whorls (Illus. 7), used for spinning yarn, which were recovered from three different sites, and the discovery of a baked clay loom-weight (Illus. 8), which is a rare find from an Irish site, suggests that weaving was carried out at Knockgraffon (site 137.1). Further evidence of craftworking came from examples of burnishing stones, which may have been used for textile production or, more likely, in leather-working.

Although there was no clear evidence that metal was being produced in or adjacent to any of the buildings excavated along the road scheme, two of the sites produced finds that indicate that metalworking was carried out in the wider area. Part of a copper-alloy object of Middle Bronze Age date was recovered from Ballydrehid (site 185.5), and fragments of a Late Bronze Age metalworking mould that had been used for casting an axehead or spearhead (Illus. 9) came from Ballylegan (site 207.2). Similarly there was no evidence that the flint artefacts (six flakes and a barbed-and-tanged arrowhead) recovered from the settlement sites had been manufactured at those locations and they had probably been discarded there after use.

Several sites had multiple broadly contemporary structures, some of which may have had non-domestic functions such as the storing of grain, the housing of animals or craft production. This is particularly relevant in the case of Knockgraffon (site 137.1), where the aforementioned loom-weight was recovered from the smaller of two buildings and may suggest that the larger structure was the main dwelling. This would parallel the archaeological evidence from Britain, where Middle Bronze Age circular buildings often occur in pairs, with the larger building being the domestic dwelling and the smaller structure being associated with craft production, particularly weaving (Ellison 1981). There may also have been a division of functions between the two roughly contemporary buildings at Ballydrehid (site 185.5), where structure A had a hearth in each of its rooms and appears to have been the main domestic dwelling, while structure B had no evidence of a hearth and may have had an ancillary function. The two quern-stone fragments recovered from the latter structure could indicate that it was used for food-processing and/or storage.

Conclusions

The 24 structures and other Bronze Age settlement evidence recorded along the N8 Cashel–Mitchelstown Road Improvement Scheme are an important addition to the archaeological record not only of Munster but of the country as a whole. The evidence shows that settlements were sited consistently in sheltered locations in areas of good land that lay in close proximity to an available water source. The structural remains recorded at these sites provide an insight into social organisation and architectural design, while the environmental evidence and material remains indicate the diet of the inhabitants and some of the activities, such as textile production, in which they engaged.

Most of the settlements were characterised by circular structures, and comparative evidence suggests that Bronze Age settlements often comprised two or more buildings. Variations in the number and layout of structures may reflect different social patterns, with single buildings representing the farmsteads of individual families and the more extensive settlements indicating larger extended family groupings. It is unlikely, however, that all of the structures on the excavated sites were dwellings; for example, some may have been granaries. Conversely, houses were probably not used exclusively for domestic activities such as eating and sleeping.

This paper has focused on the settlement evidence, but a broader view of the Bronze Age evidence recorded along the N8 Cashel–Mitchelstown Road Improvement Scheme indicates that settlement and burial sites were integrated within the contemporary landscape. Furthermore, several of the Bronze Age settlement sites demonstrate a continuity of settlement or in some cases a return to a site occupied several centuries (and in some cases millennia) previously. This may have been because the sites were ideally located or perhaps because there were ancestral ties to the site (for further discussion see McQuade et al. 2009).

Acknowledgements

The authors wish to thank the NRA archaeologists Richard O'Brien, James Eogan and Mairead McLoughlin for their contribution to the project. Thanks are due to the hard-working site staff and to the following specialists: Sara Halwas (plant remains), Lorna O'Donnell (charcoal and wood remains), Johnny Geber (human and faunal remains), Eoin Grogan and Helen Roche (pottery analysis), Conor Brady (lithics), and Siobhan Scully, Richard O'Brien and Katharina Becker (finds reports). John Sunderland photographed the finds, and Johnny Ryan and Gary Devlin prepared the graphics.

Notes

1. Ballydrehid, site 185.5: NGR 204290, 126280; height 67 m OD; excavation reg. no. E2267; ministerial direction no. A035; excavation director Melanie McQuade.

2. Knockgraffon, site 137.3: NGR 205924, 131121; height 76 m OD; excavation reg. no. E2270; ministerial direction no. A035; excavation director Colm Moriarty.

3. Ballylegan, site 207.1: NGR 208095, 125845; height 96 m OD; excavation reg. no. E2265; ministerial direction no. A035; excavation director Melanie McQuade. Ballylegan, site 207.2: NGR 208158, 125770; height 90 m OD; excavation reg. no. E2265; ministerial direction no. A035; excavation director Melanie McQuade. Cloghabreedy, site 125.1: NGR 205770 127530; height 51 m OD; excavation reg. no. E2273; ministerial direction no. A035; excavation director Colm Moriarty. Cloghabreedy, site 125.3: NGR 205900, 127450; height 49 m OD; excavation reg. no. E2273; ministerial direction no. A035; excavation director Colm Moriarty. Killemly, site 203.3: NGR 206988, 126486; height 63 m OD; excavation reg. no. E2126; ministerial direction no. A035; excavation director Melanie McQuade.

4. Ballylegan, site 207.2: NGR 208158, 125770; height 90 m OD; excavation reg. no. E2265; ministerial direction no. A035; excavation director Melanie McQuade. Ballydrehid, site 185.5: NGR E204290 N126280; height 67 m OD; excavation reg. no. E2267; ministerial direction no. A035; excavation director Melanie McQuade. Knockgraffon, site 137.3: NGR 205924, 131121; height 70 m OD; excavation reg. no. E2270; ministerial direction no. A035; excavation director Colm Moriarty. Loughfeedora, site 173.2: NGR 207400, 138213; height 113 m OD; excavation reg. no. E2292, ministerial direction no. A035; excavation director Martin Doody.

5. Knockgraffon, site 137.1: NGR 205838, 130415; height 70 m OD; excavation reg. no. E2270; ministerial direction no. A035; excavation director Colm Moriarty. Cloghabreedy, site 125.1: NGR 205770, 127530; height 51 m OD; excavation reg. no. E2273; ministerial direction no. A035; excavation director Colm Moriarty. Clonmore North, site 92.3: NGR 202085 123905; height 91 m OD; excavation reg. no. E2294; ministerial direction no. A035; excavation director Bernice Molloy.

6. Cloghabreedy, site 125.4: NGR 205840, 127850; height 50 m OD; excavation reg. no. E2274; ministerial direction no. A035; excavation director Colm Moriarty.

12. Reconstructing prehistoric and historic settlement in County Cork

Ken Hanley

"I paint objects as I think them, not as I see them"
—Pablo Picasso

Archaeology is the study of past human life, society and culture through the investigation of surviving material remains. This is an evolving process of discovery, data retrieval, data analysis, the creation of hypotheses, and ultimately the development of theories or conceptual models from which we advance our understanding of how life once was. Critical to this process are the ways in which archaeologists project their understanding of how excavated sites may originally have looked and/or functioned. This paper will focus on how the NRA have supported attempts to visually reconstruct, using computer-generated 3D modelling, some of the prehistoric and historic settlements discovered on recent national road schemes in County Cork.

The stuff of archaeology

Archaeological remains are often ephemeral—surviving only as soil discolorations, pits, post-holes, broken pieces of artefacts or other fragmentary remains. This represents an incomplete picture of what may once have been a living and thriving settlement. This is the stuff of archaeology. Archaeological excavation involves four key components: a detailed record of the archaeological remains discovered, an interpretation of that record, dissemination of both record and interpretation, and the retention of the site archive.

Seeing archaeology

So, as archaeologists, how are we visually communicating our interpreted excavation results and associated research to the general public? One of the key outcomes from any archaeological excavation is the excavation team's final interpretation of how the site may have looked and/or functioned. Visually, this is best communicated by means of some form of artistic interpretation or technical reconstruction. There is an inherent dilemma, however, in that excavations record facts based on the surviving partial remains, whereas the interpretation of the excavated remains requires some degree of conjecture so that others can see meaning. This process of combining the certain with the uncertain is part of our daily trade. In order to form a visual model of how a site may have looked originally, we are often required to merge the certainty of the excavated remains with the uncertainty of what has since perished.

the summer of 2003 by Eamonn Cotter on behalf of Archaeological Consultancy Services Ltd (ACS Ltd).[2] The Middle Bronze Age phase of the site consisted of three large subcircular enclosures (enclosures 1–3), one of which contained an oval house, and three unenclosed houses, dating broadly from 1700–1500 BC (O'Sullivan & Stanley 2005, 149). Late Bronze Age, Iron Age and medieval features were also excavated on the site (Cotter 2005).

Enclosure 1 was subcircular, measuring approximately 20 m in diameter. It was fully exposed within the southern end of the excavation area. The enclosing fencing/walls were formed by split oak timbers (c. 0.1 m thick), set upright in a narrow slot-trench and supported by large packing stones. The enclosure was entered from two points and both entrances were formed by stout posts, set approximately 1 m apart. One of the entrances was at the northern end, but angled north-east. The other was at the south-eastern end. Several sherds of Middle Bronze Age pottery were found in the slot-trench for enclosure 1. At the centre of the enclosure there was a suboval structure, possibly a house, with an internal floor space of c. 24 m² and two substantial post-holes located near the centre. These would have held posts that provided the main support for the roof. The entrance faced south-east and was clearly evident as substantial post-holes, one of which contained a fragment of a saddle quern (used for grinding grain). The apparently intentional placement of quern-stones within the structural foundations of Bronze Age houses is believed to have been intended to bring good luck to a settlement (perhaps as a votive deposit to ensure bountiful harvests).

Enclosure 2 was located to the north-west of enclosure 1. It differed from enclosure 1 in that it was enclosed by a shallow ditch rather than a fence of upright oak timbers. Only half of enclosure 2 was excavated as the other half extended beyond the road corridor, but it would appear to have been around 38 m in diameter. A causewayed entranceway was noted at the northern end. The ditch contained some sherds of Middle Bronze Age pottery. While the enclosure contained some internal features, not enough were exposed to determine its function within the overall settlement.

Enclosure 3 was located on the eastern edge of the site and only half of it was excavated. It had a diameter of approximately 22 m and was similar in construction to enclosure 1, being enclosed by a split oak timber fence. A number of small post-holes and stake-holes were excavated within the enclosure but these did not form any coherent pattern. A single sherd of Middle Bronze Age pottery was recovered from the fill of the enclosing slot-trench.

Houses B, C and D were located close together, to the north of enclosures 1 and 3. House B was subcircular with an internal floor space of approximately 49 m². It contained a concentric inner ring of six post-holes and a central post-hole that are likely to have held roof supports. Two large post-holes on the eastern side are thought to have formed part of the entrance. One of these contained a fragment of a saddle quern. House C was located c. 6 m north of house B and was almost identical in construction, with a similar floor space and internal roof supports. It appears to have been entered from the south-west. House D was 6 m east of house C. While it also contained an internal concentric ring of support posts, it differed from houses B and C in that it was oval in plan, it did not have a central support post and, more significantly, it had a distinctive porch like structure at the entrance, which faced roughly south.

The 3D digital modelling for this site attempted to capture the sense of 'village', in terms

Illus. 3—Two stills from the completed reconstruction of the Gortore 1 house, showing how multiple views can be generated from the 3D-animated reconstructions (Digitale Archäologie).

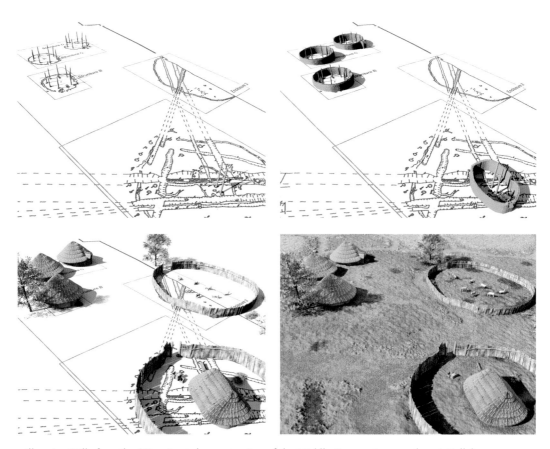

Illus. 4—Stills from the 3D-animated reconstruction of the Middle Bronze Age complex at Ballybrowney Lower 1, showing how the two-dimensional site plan is gradually brought to life (Digitale Archäologie).

of its scale, organisation and community (Illus. 4). The animated model provides a 'fly-through' that allows the viewer to visually fly around the settlement, then fly through the northern entrance to enclosure 1 and enter the enclosed central house. Once inside, the viewer is shown a scene of domestic activity (Illus. 5).

Middle Bronze Age sweathouse at Scartbarry

Scartbarry 1 was located 3.6 km north-east of the village of Watergrasshill, in a marshy area just 0.4 km south-east of the River Flesk. The site was excavated in August 2003 by Tara O'Neill (ACS Ltd).[3] What was assumed to be a classic *fulacht fiadh*, or burnt mound, proved to be the remains of a substantial and (at the time) unique sweathouse of Middle Bronze Age date. In essence, it consisted of a structure/house built over a 5-m-long stone-lined trough, with a large stone-built hearth attached to the eastern side of the trough (Illus. 6). The hearth was partly surrounded by the remains of a windbreak shelter. The entire complex appeared to be surrounded by a partially surviving shallow enclosing feature that appeared to have an entrance towards its southern edge. Charcoal from the base of the trough was radiocarbon-dated to 1650–1190 BC (Beta-201083).

The hearth measured roughly 2.3 m by 1.6 m and was composed of three thin slabs of stone laid flat. These were surrounded to the north, south and east with vertical stones forming a semicircular border to a height of approximately 0.25 m. The western edge of

Illus. 5—Interpreted scene of domestic activity inside the suboval structure within enclosure 1 at Ballybrowney Lower 1 (Digitale Archäologie).

the hearth culminated at the long stone-lined trough, which was approximately 0.5 m deep. Two large post-holes flanked the junction between the hearth and the trough. Aligned east–west, the subrectangular stone-lined trough was encircled perfectly by what would have been a timber-built and roofed oval structure/house. The sweathouse survived as an oval slot-trench with abundant packing stones. The slot-trench would originally have contained plank-built walls, encompassing a floor space of approximately 4.5 m² on either side of the trough (the total internal spatial area would have been around 16 m²). It is likely that the roof would have been covered with thatch. Overall, it was clear from the excavation that this represented a relatively permanent sweathouse, its core purpose being to trap the steam/heat derived from heated stones rolled into the trough from the connected hearth.

The 3D digital model for Scartbarry 1 aimed to visually highlight the permanent nature of the structure and the human aspects of how the site was used. The fly-through first encircled the site as a whole, then flew past the front of the sweathouse, revealing the burning hearth being tended by one individual, while several others gathered unclothed within the sweathouse itself—and all the while hot (perhaps herb-scented) steam circulates vividly within (Illus. 7).

Two Middle Bronze Age houses at Mitchelstown
Mitchelstown 1 was located 0.6 km north-west of Mitchelstown, overlooking the Gradoge River, some 0.3 km to the south. The excavation by Eamonn Cotter (Eachtra Archaeological Projects) in 2004 revealed three Middle Bronze Age houses (Tierney & Johnston, this volume), two of which were digitally remodelled (Illus. 8).[4] Based on the

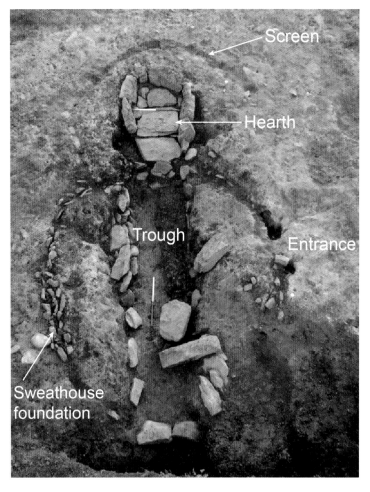

Illus. 6—Elevated view of the surviving remains of the sweathouse at Scartbarry 1 (Cork County Council).

excavated evidence, these two houses had been built over an earlier house. The two contemporary houses (A & B) were similar in construction.

House A was a roughly D-shaped structure enclosing an area of about 90 m². It was entered from the east via a 1-m-wide doorway in a slightly flattened façade. The house walls survived as a curving slot-trench, believed to have supported post-and-wattle walling. The slot-trench faded out towards the west but was likely to have formed a complete arc originally. Internally, there was a semicircular arrangement of roof support posts. The house was divided internally by a partition wall running north–south. A possible hearth was noted near the centre of the house, opposite the entrance but sheltered from it by the partition.

House B was slightly larger, with a floor area of about 120 m². It was located 1.8 m south of house A and had a similar D-shaped plan and eastern entrance. The slot-trench was found only around the northern half of the house and it was unclear to the excavator whether it ever existed around the remainder of the house, although it may have. Like house A, it also had a semicircular arrangement of internal post-holes that acted as main roof supports, but, unlike house A, there was no evidence of an internal dividing wall nor of a recognisable hearth.

The 3D digital model for Mitchelstown 1 focused on the 'rural farmstead' nature of the site (see Tierney & Johnston, Chapter 10, Illus 7). The viewer first 'flies' around the site, then approaches and enters house A. Inside, the partition hints at a dual purpose of private and more public access—the hearth indicating the private section.

Illus. 7—Still from the reconstruction of the sweathouse at Scartbarry 1 (Digitale Archäologie).

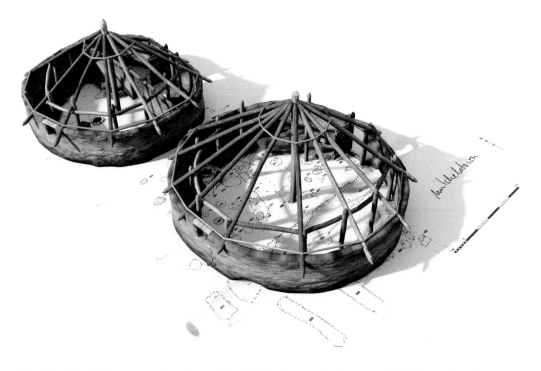

Illus. 8—3D digital reconstruction of two of the Middle Bronze Age houses at Mitchelstown 1 under way
(Digitale Archäologie)

Medieval moated site at Ballinvinny South

The site at Ballinvinny South was located near the crest of a moderately steep west-facing slope, overlooking an unnamed tributary of the Butlerstown River, c. 7 km north of Cork Harbour. The site, which was excavated in 2001 by Eamonn Cotter on behalf of Sheila Lane & Associates, consisted of a subrectangular moated enclosure with two internal rectangular houses.[5]

The moat ditch was generally steep-sided with a flat-bottomed profile. It varied from 2.8 m to 1.7 m in width and from 1.15 m to 0.58 m in depth. A linear ditch appears to have fed spring water into the moat ditch from higher ground to the east. According to the excavator, it seemed likely that the moat would have filled only partially (and perhaps seasonally). A 5.5-m-wide entrance was located at the south side of the enclosure. Here, three surviving post-holes may have been the remnants of an entrance gate. Immediately east of the entrance was an 8 m section of drystone wall against the inner (north) side of the moat cut. This revetment was interpreted as a support for an earthen entrance embankment that may have served as a platform, guarding the entranceway.

Two rectangular structures (structures A and B) were excavated within the enclosure. Structure A measured 11 m by 4 m and was aligned north–south. Foundation trenches partly survived for the north, south and east walls of the structure, while pairs of post-holes formed the north-western and south-western corners. Little evidence for the western wall survived. Clay-bonded stone foundations were uncovered within the interior north-eastern corner of structure A. These appeared to have been the remains of a stone chimney.

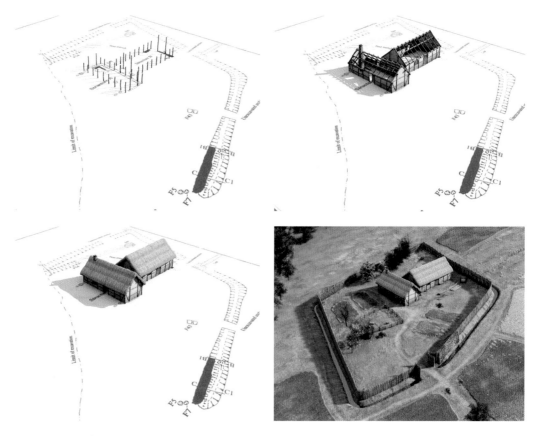

Illus. 9—Stills from the 3D-animated reconstruction of the medieval moated site at Ballinvinny South, showing how the two-dimensional site plan is gradually brought to life (Digitale Archäologie).

Structure B lay immediately east of, and was equal in size to, structure A. It was aligned east–west. A section of the east foundation wall survived as a few courses of clay-bonded stone. A sherd of late 13th/early 14th-century Saintonge pottery was found within material backfilled into the foundation trench. While some evidence for the northern and southern foundation trenches survived, more recent ground disturbance appears to have largely obliterated the interior of the structure and the western wall foundations.

The 3D digital model for Ballinvinny South tried to capture the overall look of the site based on the excavated evidence (Illus. 9). Again, the viewer first 'flies' around the site, then enters through the entranceway before encircling the internal structures, at least one of which (structure A) is likely to have been domestic (Illus. 10).

Illus. 10—Still from the 'fly-through' of the reconstruction of the Ballinvinny South moated site, approaching entrance (Digitale Archäologie).

Challenges and opportunities

In this exercise in 3D-animated modelling of archaeological sites, the excavation directors were faced with several challenges, most notably the need to make conjectures based on only partial remains. The initial unease expressed by site directors was based on professional integrity: there was some reluctance to stand over unproven conjecture. This is a widespread challenge; all too often archaeologists tend, by habit, to think almost exclusively in two dimensions. Often the only third dimension discussed is the depth of surviving cut features. If we consider that perhaps less than 5% of the material remains that once occupied a settlement site might survive to the time of excavation, a 3D digital model of the site would therefore require 95% of the site to be remodelled from the surviving 5% of remains. This is done by comparison, experience, consultation, intuition and a degree of artistic licence.

Another source of unease for many site directors stems from the particular circumstances of Irish archaeology, whereby, given the commercial nature of development-led contracts, individual directors may be charged with excavating a Neolithic house one month and a 17th-century kiln the next month. This reality, of a mobile work market and development-dominated contracts, has meant that a director excavating one or more Bronze Age houses is not necessarily an expert on all matters relating to the Bronze Age. There is therefore a natural uncertainty concerning issues such as what appropriate Bronze Age house furnishings, styles of dress or contemporary farming practices should be depicted.

In Ireland there is relatively little shared experience in formulating detailed models of how sites may have looked. It is for this reason that many choose to shy away from anything other than perhaps safe and stylised artistic impressions. Detailed 3D digital animations force us away from our traditional comfort zones owing to the sheer precision offered by digital media. With current and future 3D (and indeed 4D) modelling, the ball is firmly in our court and we now have the opportunity to flex our creative and intellectual muscles in terms of testing our hypotheses of how ancient structures may have looked in precise technical/architectural detail and how sites may have looked in terms of their social/cultural/landscape 'scene'. Equally, the interpolation of disparate datasets across software platforms allows for more integrated manipulation of information. What is required is a degree of coordination, so that virtual landscapes can be developed that creatively incorporate collections of digital data. If our aim as archaeologists is to study the past, then we need to address the imbalance between the archaeological record, which involves vast data banks, and archaeological interpretation, which involves the clear presentation of our evolving ideas with the gaps filled in.

Acknowledgements

I would like to clearly acknowledge the primary work of the featured excavation directors, namely Eamonn Cotter (Ballybrowney Lower 1, Mitchelstown 1 and Ballinvinny South), Tara O'Neill (Scartbarry 1) and Julianna O'Donoghue (Gortore 1), and of Matthias Link and his team at Digitale Archäologie, Germany. All modelling was carried out by Digitale Archäologie using Autodesk 3D Max Version 9.

Notes

1. Gortore 1: NGR 181815, 101661; height 39 m OD; ministerial direction no. A014; excavation director Julianna O'Donoghue.
2. Ballybrowney Lower 1: NGR 179146, 90645; height 71 m OD; excavation licence no. 03E1058; excavation director Eamonn Cotter.
3. Scartbarry 1: NGR 178392, 87553; height 112 m OD; excavation licence no. 03E1438; excavation director Tara O'Neill.
4. Mitchelstown 1: NGR 180869, 113639; height 106 m OD; excavation licence no. 04E1072; excavation director Eamonn Cotter.
5. Ballinvinny South: NGR 173989, 079790; height 94 m OD; excavation licence no. 01E 0111; excavation director Eamonn Cotter.

13. Camlin 3: a cemetery-settlement in north Tipperary

Colm Flynn

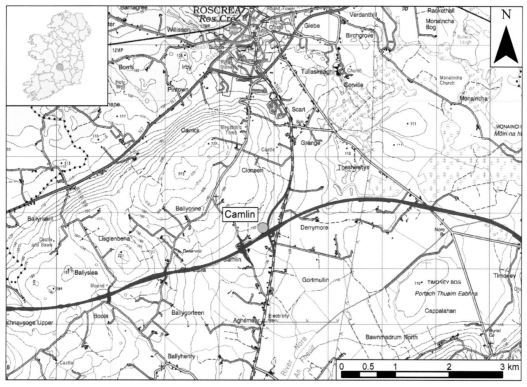

Illus. 1—Location of the cemetery-settlement at Camlin 3, Co. Tipperary (based on the Ordnance Survey Ireland map).

Camlin 3, c. 3 km south of Roscrea town, Co. Tipperary, was located on the east-facing slope of a natural ridge of high ground that runs from the Devil's Bit mountain range south-west of Camlin to Roscrea in the north (Illus. 1). The location has commanding views to the east and south-east and overlooks bogland immediately to the east. Camlin was situated close to the important early medieval routeway known as Slíghe Dála. The well-known Early Christian monastic site at Moinaincha is less than 3 km to the north-east, and a known archaeological site at Camlin is described as a levelled 'Ringfort (possible, site)' (Record of Monuments and Places no. TN017-031) in the *Archaeological Inventory of County Tipperary* (Farrelly & O'Brien 2002, 85). Archaeological testing by Valerie J Keeley Ltd in advance of the construction phase of the N7 Castletown–Nenagh: Derrinsallagh to Ballintotty road scheme confirmed the presence of a large archaeological site at the location of the known monument, and several other concentrations of prehistoric and historic archaeological features were also identified. These features were excavated subsequently by Valerie J Keeley Ltd in July 2007–July 2008 on behalf of Laois County Council and the NRA.[1] On excavation the possible ringfort was shown to be the remains of a so-called 'cemetery-settlement', an early medieval site type that has been identified on numerous road schemes throughout the country in recent years (e.g. Seaver 2006; O'Neill 2007; O'Sullivan 2007b, 90–3; Clarke & Carlin 2008).

The cemetery-settlement

Approximately half the area of the monument described in the *Inventory* was affected by the road project, whilst the other half remains undisturbed under pasture fields (Illus. 2 & 3). A ditch and remnants of an internal bank forming a subcircular enclosure were identified by excavation. Within the excavated area the interior of the enclosure measured 42 m north-east–south-west and 24 m north–south. Including the ditch, the entire enclosure measured 50 m north-east–south-west. The bank had been mostly destroyed in recent times but measured approximately 3.5 m in width and survived to a height of 0.25 m. Owing to disturbance of the underlying archaeology by later agricultural activity, the bank material contained slag, iron knife blades and a large quantity of animal bone and disarticulated human bone.

The enclosure ditch varied in size, from 6 m wide and 2.2 m deep in the south-west to 1.9 m deep and 5 m wide in the north-east. At its lower levels the ditch fills were waterlogged, resulting in the preservation of a number of wooden artefacts. Although no break was identified in the ditch in the excavated area, it became shallower to the north. A geophysical survey carried out in the field immediately north of the excavation area identified a potential entrance in the north-east quadrant of the enclosure (Illus. 4). Near the western end of the excavated portion of the ditch a crouched inhumation burial of an adult male was identified, lying west–east within a pit grave cut into the fill of the ditch

Illus. 2—Elevated view of Camlin 3, looking south-west (AirShots Ltd).

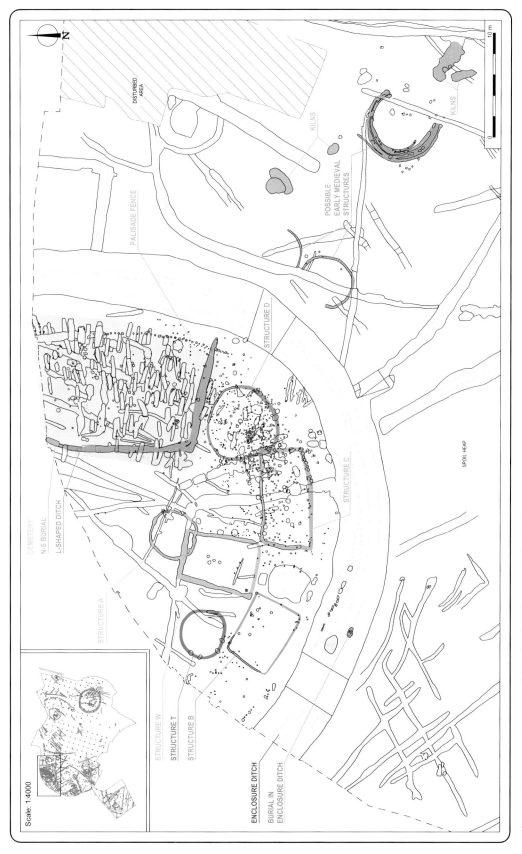

Illus. 3—Post-excavation plan of Camlin 3 (Valerie J Keeley Ltd).

Illus. 4—Greyscale image of the results of geophysical survey at Camlin 3 (J M Leigh Surveys Ltd/Valerie J Keeley Ltd).

approximately 0.3 m above its base. Further east along the ditch at the same level a possible wooden bowstave and three narrow wooden rods were found, each about 2 m in length. Other finds from the lower levels of the ditch included sharpening stones, iron knife blades, bone pins and a decorated bone spindle-whorl.

When the spread of disturbed bank material was excavated at the eastern side of the enclosure, a cemetery and a north–south-aligned palisade fence line became apparent (Illus. 2 & 3). The bank material sealed the easternmost graves, indicating that it may have post-dated the cemetery. First edition Ordnance Survey maps of the area, drafted in the 1830s, depict a bank at this location, indicating that it was visible until modern times. A bank and ditch are the principal elements of a ringfort; the identification of graves under the bank, however, provided evidence of a potential pre-ringfort phase at the site. A number of the graves had destroyed earlier post-holes, some of which were part of the palisade. Other post-holes truncated by graves were related to activity earlier than the cemetery. This sequence provides three phases of activity at the site: a primary phase consisting of post-holes possibly related to unidentified structures, a secondary phase consisting of the establishment of a cemetery, including graves that destroyed some of the earlier post-holes, and a third phase marked by the creation of a large bank that extended over the easternmost graves. The bank was presumably contemporary with the creation of the large enclosure ditch, which would have produced the soil required for the bank. It is possible that the enclosure ditch identified in the course of the excavation had superseded an earlier, smaller ditch, which could have been contemporary with the cemetery and the earlier post-holes.

The graveyard was defined by an L-shaped ditch, which, at its eastern limit, terminated 2 m short of the enclosure ditch. As it continued outside the excavation area to the north it became narrower and shallower. We can assume that this ditch was originally intended as a boundary around the graveyard but became obsolete as the community's need for burial space grew. This L-shaped ditch was subsequently backfilled and was cut by a row of later graves. At Mount Offaly, Cabinteely, Co. Dublin, Conway (2000) identified enclosing ditches around an early medieval cemetery. These ditches also had graves cutting their fills, similar to Camlin 3. The main concentration of burials was contained within the area defined by the L-shaped ditch. Some graves, however, were situated outside this area to the south, where they cut archaeological features within the interior of an earlier subcircular structure (structure D).

In total 151 human burials were excavated in the cemetery. Overall, the state of preservation of most of the skeletal remains was poor. As some of the grave-cuts were very shallow and a large quantity of disarticulated human bone was recovered during the excavation of the enclosure, it is likely that the total number of burials was originally greater. The burials appeared to continue northwards outside the excavation area, so the total number of skeletons in this cemetery cannot be established without further archaeological investigation.

What is clear from the excavated graves is that the people interred at Camlin 3 were Christian; all except one were interred in the traditonal Christian manner, lying west–east (with the head to the west). Whilst a minority were flexed burials, the majority were extended supine. Several graves had evidence of stone cobbles lining the sides of the grave, others had possible stone 'ear muffs' against the sides of the skull, and one had evidence of plank lining. Grave-goods were identified in a minority of cases, and slag was found in several grave fills. Over 20 grave fills contained one heavily corroded iron nail or pin, which

Illus. 5—Glass beads recovered from the grave of a juvenile burial (John Sunderland).

may suggest the presence of burial shrouds. Knife blades or other iron tools (possibly awls) were found at the right hip of five extended adult skeletons. This suggests the presence of a belt, on which the knife or tool hung. Four blue glass beads and one white bead were found with the poorly preserved skeleton of a juvenile (Illus. 5).

One skeleton was not interred according to typical Christian burial traditions. This individual was buried in a grave cut into the L-shaped ditch, 13.5 m west of the enclosure ditch, in effect on the boundary or periphery of the communal graveyard. The skeleton was of an adult, was in a crouched position and was aligned north–south, with the head at the south, typical of a pre-Christian burial tradition. Several explanations for this anomaly can be suggested: the deceased was from outside the community, suffered from a perceived abnormality, had committed a crime, or was not Christian, living in a mostly Christian community.

In total six structures were identified within the enclosure (Illus. 3). Two were circular or subcircular (structures A and D) and three were rectangular (structures B, C and W). The shape of the sixth structure (structure T) was unclear but it was probably subcircular. Structure A was circular, measured 5 m in diameter and may have functioned as a domestic dwelling. It was located centrally within the enclosure and was stratigraphically the earliest structure identified. A linear ditch that was probably contemporary with structure A was truncated by structural elements of structure C. Structure T was approximately 5 m in diameter. Later linear features that truncated structure T also truncated structure A, suggesting that these structures may have been contemporary.

Structure D was subcircular and measured 7 m in diameter. It contained numerous stake-holes that occurred in clusters, two of which were around hearths, while one cluster was aligned south-east–north-west, possibly functioning as an internal screen dividing the structure for distinct purposes. Structure D also contained several pits, presumably for storage; the largest and deepest of these contained an almost complete set of red deer antlers, with several points missing. Worked antler points were found in both structure C (see below) and structure D, as well as in the enclosure ditch fills. Several decorated animal bone and horn artefacts were retrieved from contemporary features internal and external to structure D. Two of these bone artefacts appear to have functioned as handles for metal tools. Structure D may have been a multi-purpose building providing space for domestic activity and possibly specialised bone-working.

Structure B was 7.5 m long and 5.5 m wide. The foundations were shallower than those forming the other five structures within the enclosure, suggesting that it may have had a more temporary purpose than the other structures.

Structure W was 5 m long and 4 m wide and had an entrance in its southern wall. The eastern wall was situated close to the north-western corner of structure C, which indicates that these structures may have been contemporary.

Structure C was an east–west-aligned rectangular building and was situated 2.5 m north of the enclosure ditch. A concentration of material associated with metal- and bone-working was located in the south-east quadrant of the enclosure. Structure C may have functioned as a work-shed related to metalworking; evidence of smelting and possible secondary smithing was found at its eastern end. This consisted of complete and damaged knives as well as slag and hammerscale (a by-product of smithing consisting of tiny fragments of metal, which are often found in the immediate vicinity of the smithing hearth and anvil). The northern wall of structure C was situated over an earlier inhumation burial, one of the westernmost burials, possibly related to the final phase of burials.

Stratigraphically the circular structures appeared to pre-date the rectangular structures. As stated previously, ditches related to structure A were earlier than the foundation elements of structure C. The northern foundation trench of structure W truncated the slot-trench forming structure A. While structure C post-dated one of the westernmost burials of the cemetery, other graves disturbed layers of occupational debris within the interior of structure D, indicating that they post-dated the abandonment of this structure.

The relationship of structures B, C and D with the enclosure ditch and bank is unclear. Before structure C was identified, a 0.2-m-thick layer of bank material and a bank foundation layer of stony, redeposited natural clay were excavated. These layers sealed structure C, suggesting that the creation of the bank post-dated the abandonment of the structure. Metalworking features which were probably contemporary with structure C were truncated by the enclosure ditch and were also sealed by the bank foundation layer and bank material. The skeletons that were found within the interior of structure D post-dated it and were also sealed by the bank material. It is possible that the bank and enclosure ditch post-dated the cemetery and the identified structures if, as has been previously suggested, the enclosure ditch replaced an earlier smaller ditch. This bank and ditch could have formed a later ringfort, with the focus of its activities possibly lying outside the area of excavation.

To the east and south of the enclosure other features and structures were identified. Most of these structures were partially enclosed by a network of double ditches, and some were located near cereal-drying kilns. Some of these features are quite probably contemporary with the enclosure and cemetery. They provide us with a picture of a substantial early medieval community working the land, raising cattle, hunting deer, making knives and

Illus. 6—Decorated silver and bronze dress-pin. The ring is 17 mm in diameter (Valerie J Keeley Ltd).

other metal objects, and trading with skilled exponents of other crafts. Items such as a silver and bronze decorated dress-pin, which was retrieved from within the enclosure ditch, may have required a level of skill too advanced to have been manufactured at this site (Illus. 6).

Conclusion

The siting of a cemetery within a settlement has until recently been considered quite rare in an Irish archaeological context. Recent excavations at Knowth (Stout & Stout 2008) identified an early medieval 'secular cemetery' that was superseded by an early medieval enclosure. Although there is evidence at Camlin 3 for activity prior to the cemetery, it is highly likely that the L-shaped ditch demarcating the cemetery also allowed contemporary non-burial activities to take place in its environs. The presence of slag in some grave fills indicates that metalworking may have been taking place when the cemetery was still in use. This provides us with evidence of domestic and possibly industrial activity occurring contemporarily with a functioning cemetery.

At Ballykilmore, Co. Westmeath, post-holes belonging to an earlier wooden structure were identified beneath a rectangular stone-built church (Channing & Randolph-Quinney 2006). It is possible that these post-holes were part of an earlier church. At Camlin 3 structure C was also rectangular, formed by wooden posts and, similar to medieval churches, aligned east–west. We have no definitive evidence of ecclesiastical activity at Camlin 3, however, and no evidence that structure C performed a religious function, while the abundance of domestic artefacts indicates that Camlin 3 was solely a secular settlement and cemetery. It is known that secular Christian cemeteries were in use in Ireland from the arrival of Christianity in the mid-fifth century and were still in use in the eighth and possibly the ninth century (O'Brien 1992).

At Camlin 3 we have identified structures that potentially pre-date this secular cemetery (structure A and possibly structures D and T). It is also possible that structure D was contemporary with some of the earlier burials but pre-dated later burials. Structures C, B and W could post-date the cemetery, and this would explain the truncation of an earlier grave by the slot-trench of structure C. A final phase of archaeological activity at Camlin 3 could be represented by the deepening and widening of a pre-existing ditch and the creation of an internal bank.

Archaeologists rarely get an opportunity to excavate the environs of a large site, identifying potentially related dwellings and features. At Camlin 3 we have identified 12 structures (six internal and six external) that we believe are related to the early medieval phase of activity. Scientific dating will either confirm our suppositions or cause us to reinterpret them. But it is possible that at Camlin 3 we have identified the holding of a successful early medieval *bóaire* (prosperous farmer) (Kelly 2000, 23), or someone of even higher status. The cemetery could represent the familial burial place. The structures outside the enclosure could represent the dwellings of his bonded servants, the *dóer* (unfree servants) (ibid., 11). Taking into account the possibility that other ringforts and enclosures in the area may also have had external dwellings (the *Archaeological Inventory* lists 27 ringforts and 14 enclosures within 6 km of Camlin) and may also have been contemporary with the early medieval site at Camlin 3, the cemetery at Camlin 3 may have been used by a substantial rural community in a time when religious influence had not yet ensured that the deceased were interred in consecrated ground.

Acknowledgements

Over 50 people were involved in the excavation at Camlin 3, and grateful thanks are owed to all of them. Site Supervisors Paolo Ciuchini, Eileen McKenna, Malachy Byrne and Agata Raclaw deserve special mention, as do Oscar Ryan and Lukasz Konopinski for the illustrations. Thanks also to Senior Archaeologist Eamon Cotter, Logistics Manager Fiona MacCauliffe and staff at Valerie J Keeley Ltd.

Note

1. NGR 213798, 185726; height 140 m OD; excavation reg. no. E3580; ministerial direction no. A038; RMP no. TN017–031.

14. Wining and dining in a medieval village at Mullaghmast, Co. Kildare

Angus Stephenson

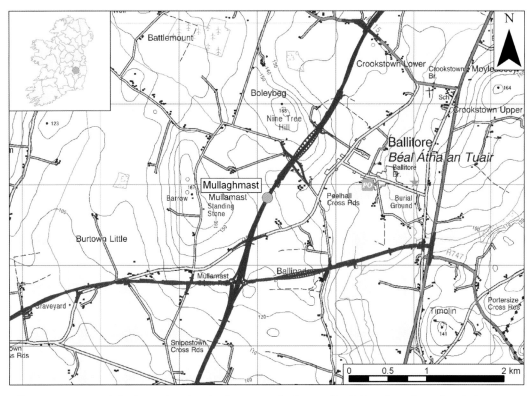

Illus. 1—Location of the deserted medieval village at Mullaghmast, Co. Kildare (based on the Ordnance Survey Ireland map).

The site of Mullaghmast, Co. Kildare, was identified as having archaeological potential in the Environmental Impact Assessment for the N9/N10 Kilcullen–Waterford Scheme: Kilcullen to Carlow because of its proximity to a potential medieval castle site (Record of Monuments and Places no. KD036-018). A geophysical survey within the proposed road corridor (Bartlett 2002) and aerial photographs of the route (taken by Markus Casey on behalf of the NRA) revealed a number of features of probable archaeological origin. This was confirmed subsequently by test-trenching (Bayley 2006), and full excavation of a 45-m-wide corridor running for c. 400 m through the site was undertaken in April–December 2007.[1] The archaeological investigations were conducted on behalf of Kildare County Council and the NRA and resulted in the discovery of a deserted medieval village comprising building foundations, stone and clay occupation surfaces and industrial remains, such as kilns, hearths and furnaces, within a tenement plot framework defined by roads and boundary and drainage ditches, with water features such as wells, stream channels and a pond.

Post-excavation assessment and analysis are at a very early stage at the time of writing. This paper is therefore intended to provide a broad, and necessarily provisional, picture of what was found and to give an outline indication of some of the directions which subsequent research may take, using the evidence from c. 2,500 written context records and more than 10,000 associated individual finds.

Early history and archaeological remains

The site lay on the north-facing slope of a low hill, rising to c. 140 m above sea level, in the southern part of County Kildare (Illus. 1 & 2). Approximately 1 km to the west, a large ringfort, the Rath of Mullaghmast, sits on the brow of an escarpment overlooking the broad, flat valley of the River Barrow (Illus. 3). The excavation site and the ringfort were easily visible from each other. The ringfort was a long-established and conspicuous landmark from well before the Norman invasions, appearing several times in Early Christian annals as a local tribal capital and meeting place (Fitzgerald 1895, 379).

After the first Anglo-Norman invasions in AD 1169, this part of southern Kildare was granted by Strongbow to Walter de Ridelisford I (whose name has several variant spellings and who had a son of the same name), who received the substantial territory of 20 knight's fees in Omurethi (Mulally 2002, II, 3096–8), which has been identified as the tribal territory of the Uí Muiredaigh, of which the O'Tooles were lords (Orpen 2005, 146). Brooks (1952b, 118) dates the original disposition to 1173. As the colonising settlement gathered momentum with the defeat of the O'Tooles in 1177–8, de Ridelisford sought to establish control by constructing castles and planting colonists in southern Kildare (O'Byrne 2003, 17). The continuation of this activity saw the foundation of castles in the early 1180s at Castledermot and Kilkea, both properties controlled by the de Ridelisfords (Orpen 2005, 146). Although there is evidence supporting the existence of a later castle at Mullaghmast, no trace of an early motte-and-bailey-type earthen fortification was found during the excavations.

The basic layout of the settlement seems to have been planned from the outset, with a central crossroads and defining boundary ditches around the village (Illus. 4). The roads and ditches within it had the effect of dividing the settlement into zones, which were modified substantially several times during its existence. The stratigraphic evolution of the site is likely to be well dated by an assemblage of approximately 10,000 sherds of medieval pottery, found scattered over the whole site in all types of features and layers, including those disturbed by later agricultural activity. A preliminary assessment of this assemblage suggests that a high proportion of it dates from the 12th and 13th centuries, comprising Leinster Cooking Ware and other local wares, with a scattering of foreign imports from England and France (A Kyle, pers. comm.). Substantial numbers of metal finds and a range of household objects were also recovered.

The contemporary writer Giraldus Cambrensis, who was related to Walter de Ridelisford I through a shared grandmother, famously commented that Ireland

'. . . has not, and never had, vines and their cultivators. Imported wines, however, conveyed in the ordinary commercial way, are so abundant that you would scarcely notice that the vine was neither cultivated nor gave its fruit there. Poitou out of its own superabundance sends plenty of wine, and Ireland is pleased to send in return the hides of animals and the skins of flocks and wild animals' (O'Meara 1982, 35).

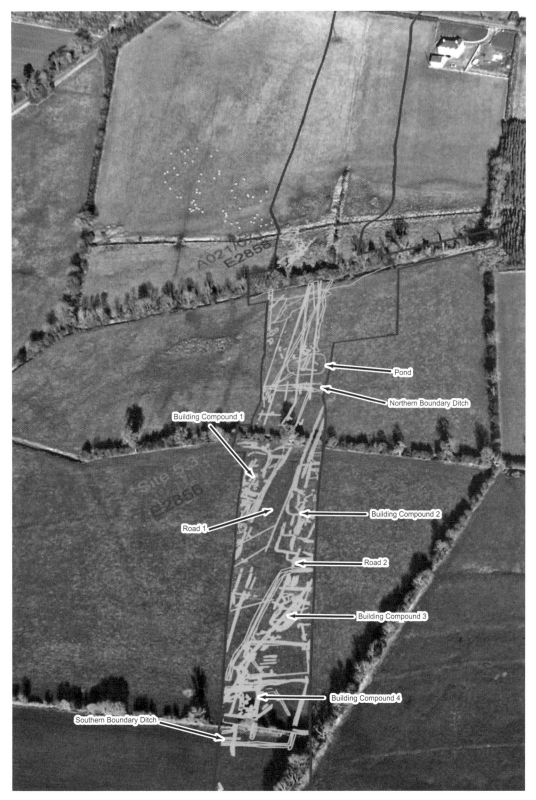

Illus. 2—Pre-excavation aerial view of the site from the south, with the post-excavation survey overlaid (features shown in yellow). The neighbouring fields suggest evidence of the extent of the deserted village (Headland Archaeology Ltd/Markus Casey).

Illus. 3—Part of the deserted medieval village under excavation in the foreground, with the Rath of Mullaghmast on the horizon in the background (AirShots Ltd).

Illus. 4—Medieval road with side ditches leading into the centre of the village from the north (Headland Archaeology Ltd).

Illus. 5—Boundary ditch at northern edge of village with pond beyond (AirShots Ltd).

It seems likely that the analysis of the pottery assemblage from this site, which includes many recognisable fragments from baluster-type glazed jugs, will show evidence of such trading contact between Ireland and France. The most likely route by which wine would have arrived in Kildare would be by the River Barrow, 9 km to the west at Athy, via Waterford rather than Dublin. An incidental detail that might support the suggestion of such river transport was the presence on site of oyster shells. These are not at all uncommon on medieval sites, particularly near the coast, but Mullaghmast's location some 25 miles inland suggests that considerable effort would have been needed to deliver them.

The site sloped down sharply at the northern end and a series of springs on the slope fed a number of streams at the bottom of it. Their meandering former courses were clearly visible and contained medieval pottery in their fills.

The bounds of the occupied part of the settlement were established by two substantial east–west-aligned, V-profiled ditches, approximately 240 m apart. Between the northernmost of these ditches and the streams lay a small pond measuring c. 25 m by 20 m across (Illus. 5). Ponds were frequently maintained in medieval settlements for a variety of purposes, one of which was the holding of fresh fish before consumption (Hammond 1993, 23). This pond may have been initially formed and filled by one of the springs on the slope, but it appears to have been managed using a ditch running very close to it. Gravel pathways were also traceable from the village to the pond and beyond to the streams.

This pond contained a sedimentary sequence with peat layers and medieval pottery, but the most conspicuous finds were several deer antlers at the bottom of it amongst dumped timbers. It seems likely that these were the product of hunting or butchery, but the possibility remains that the antler tines were collected after natural shedding for conversion

Illus. 6—Medieval stone foundations under excavation, with Leinster Cooking Ware pottery (Headland Archaeology Ltd).

into artefacts. Antlers need to be soaked before carving (MacGregor 1985), and these finds may be evidence of craftworking as well as diet. Walter de Ridelisford II was granted the hunting privilege of 'free warren' for manors including Kilkea in 1226 (Brooks 1952b, 135), and arrowheads and large dogs' (or wolves') teeth recovered from the site might support the hunting hypothesis.

A roughly square area c. 20–25 m across, midway between the village's boundary ditches, appeared to have been left open deliberately and was never built over. To the north of this space, a compacted slightly cambered surface lay on the interface with the glacial till, with side ditches to the east and west. This ran diagonally, from north-east to south-west, across the site for c. 80 m, with the side ditches converging slightly to the north. A similar layout was evident on the eastern and southern sides of the central area. The full effect appears to represent a village-green type of space at the centre of the settlement at a crossroads. The roadways with flanking drainage ditches approached this area from all sides.

The north-east–south-west-running roadway in the northern part of the site defined triangular areas on both sides of it within the road corridor, although the original plots would have been of a different shape. A complex and evolving series of ditches marked out the settlement plots within them. There were ditched enclosures at the northern end of the settlement backing on to the major boundary ditch, with building plots between them slightly up the slope on the flatter areas. On the eastern side of the road at least two phases of building took place, whilst on the western side there were at least three. Within the plots, buildings appear in the first instance to have been formed as clay-and-timber or wattle-and-daub structures, with beaten clay floor surfaces. Some features have been identified as post-holes, stake-holes and sill-beams, but the evidence they supply for the plans of the structures is very incomplete. These sequences are likely to produce better evidence for the use of space within the village than for details of the construction of the buildings.

On the western side of the northern road, the buildings were physically extended over the earliest ditch, which had been backfilled. At its southern end, a 1.2-m-wide stone-packed foundation with an internal clay floor ran parallel to the ditch before being linked to another curved foundation over it (Illus. 6). These foundations could have supported a very substantial structure. Road metalling ran up to a cobbled gap c. 1.5 m wide at the buildings' southern end, representing an entranceway into the main part of the structure. To the south another foundation, represented by a double line of rocks parallel to the original roadside ditch, was recorded for a further 8 m. There was little evidence for the use of mortar in any part of the site, suggesting that some buildings may have been constructed using a drystone-walling technique combined with timber and clay.

At some point this access route was altered by backfilling the ditches and covering them with a dense stone surface: the ditches of the roadway running downhill from the south would have flooded the green. A much larger ditch, c. 2 m wide and between 1 m and 1.5 m deep, was dug, linking to the ditch running eastwards downhill from the green. The north–south ditch was excavated for a distance of c. 75 m, and a further large ditch coming off it at right angles to the east near its exposed centre was excavated for c. 35 m.

When combined with the southern boundary ditch of the settlement, these ditches marked out two large separate compounds. The basic layout of each of them may have been roughly similar, with a metalled access road or path on the west side between the ditch and the buildings and individual plots defined within them by further ditches. The original setting out seems to have involved plots roughly 5 m² being marked out and later extended, although this scheme is more applicable to an interpretation of the southern compound than the central one, which was radically realigned on at least one occasion.

The southern compound measured c. 70 m from north to south and enclosed a series of buildings fronting onto the edge of the trackway beside the western ditch. These buildings were set at the western ends of a series of ditched enclosures, with an alleyway behind them and a matching series of workshop areas set back across the lane. To the east a series of parallel ditches crossed the site to meet the eastern arm of the southern boundary ditch. A large hearth was excavated in one of the rear workshops and another had been truncated by a modern field boundary ditch. The area to the north of the buildings contained numerous intercutting linear features, most of which appeared to be attempts to improve drainage.

The central compound was similar to the southern one but was more obviously concerned with industrial activities, with a realigned, partially stone-revetted, ditch arrangement involving a central water-filled pool. Features in this area included a keyhole-shaped cereal-drying kiln, with a windbreak and a possible clamp (another type of temporary kiln); a stone-lined pit in a ditched enclosure, with an extensive spread of charcoal, ash and stake-holes; a deep enclosure ditch filled with charcoal and ash; and a large hearth standing separately in its own enclosure. This hearth lay over a square-shaped cut, which was 3 m across with rounded corners, and a stone foundation beside it, measuring c. 2 m long by 1 m wide. The design of these compounds suggests a division of labour supervised by a central authority within the settlement, as they were subjected to large-scale cross-compound realignment at least twice during their occupation.

Illus. 7—Silver long-cross penny of King Edward I (19 mm in diameter), minted in Canterbury between 1294 and 1299 (Headland Archaeology Ltd).

Five larger pits were excavated across the site. These had been dug down to the water-table and are thought to have been wells. In the backfill of one of these, a silver long-cross penny of King Edward I was found (Illus. 7); this was minted in Canterbury between 1294 and 1299. Its deposition here suggests a point in time when the well in this part of the site went out of use.

Later history and abandonment

Walter de Ridelisford II died in approximately 1240. He had two daughters: Emmeline, who first married Hugh de Lacy, Earl of Ulster, then Stephen de Longespee, subsequently justiciar of Ireland; and Margaret, who married Robert de Marisco (or Mariscis). Margaret and Robert had a daughter, Christiana, and after a series of family deaths a jury's inquisition into the land deeds concluded that she, at the age of about seven, was the heir of both her father Robert de Marisco and her grandfather Walter de Ridelisford II in 1244 (Brooks 1952b; 1931–2). After marrying Ebulo de Geneva at the age of eleven and becoming widowed soon afterwards, Christiana and her sister Eleanor controlled lands scattered across Ireland from Bray to Galway. In 1280 she made an arrangement with King Edward I and Queen Eleanor to exchange her lands in Ireland for their equivalents in England. The situation was complicated further by the death of Queen Eleanor in 1290, after which another arrangement was made, whereby Christiana took an interest for life from Edward in some of her Irish properties again, with a reversion when she died to Maurice Fitzmaurice Fitzgerald, who had married Christiana's niece Emmeline. By a series of transactions involving the maintenance of moieties, or shares, in the lands, it fell to the justiciar of Edward I, Sir John Wogan, to consolidate all of these interests in 1305, including 'all the lands and tenements in Kilkea and Tristledermot [Castledermot] which the king had of the gift of Christiana de Marisco, to hold for ten years at a rent of £40 a year' (Sweetman & Handcock 1886, quoted in Brooks 1952a, 53). By this means Wogan obtained direct control of the Uí Muiredaigh estates of the de Ridelisfords, which descended to his heirs for several generations (Devitt 1916). Christiana de Marisco died without issue in 1312, and King Edward II confirmed the grant of all the lands of Kilkea and Castledermot to Wogan in 1317 (Morrin 1861, 21).

The dates are significant because this was a particularly turbulent period in Irish history. In the early 14th century the military situation for the Anglo-Normans in Leinster was precarious, and the River Barrow frontier was 'in a state of collapse' (O'Byrne 2003, 82). The Irish resurgence against the Anglo-Normans had begun in the later 13th century, and there were continual outbreaks of hostilities both to the east and west of County Kildare (Orpen 2005, 440–60; O'Byrne 2003, 58–86). To make matters worse, Edward Bruce invaded Ireland in 1315 with an army from Scotland, and in the campaign at the end of this year the armies of both sides would have passed very close to Mullaghmast between Castledermot and the battlefield of Ardscull a short distance to the north-west.

At a time when the Anglo-Normans were suffering from severe taxation and purveyance burdens to finance costly foreign ventures in Wales, Scotland and France, a series of bad harvests caused by heavy rainfall at critical times resulted in famines, outbreaks of sheep and cattle murrain, and plague amongst a weakened population. These are recorded in many places in the Irish Annals, but in the worst years of 1315–16 famine was widespread throughout the whole of western Europe (Prestwich 2005, 439). Edward Bruce had to curtail operations at times through inability to feed his army by ravaging the countryside in the usual manner of medieval warfare. The final catastrophe of this period arrived with the outbreak of the plague known as the Black Death in 1348–9. It might be expected that a peasant community living in an exposed nucleated settlement amongst an increasingly hostile native population would be particularly vulnerable, and it appears that the vast majority of the finds from the village site date from before the late 14th century, suggesting at least a severe decline in prosperity after that time, if not complete destruction or abandonment.

Mullaghmast, however, puts in later historical appearances when royal military services, presumably to deal with specific local problems, were requested in 1422−3 and 1430 (Otway-Ruthven 1980, 362−9; Frame 1996). This implies that the location was at least recognisable for the musters of temporary militia. Perhaps the explanation is that the castle remained inhabited whilst the village faded away. The archaeological and historical records for the site will be used during the post-excavation analysis to try to cast light on the stages of such a process.

The castle appears for the last time on the Noble and Keenan map of 1752. On the Alexander Taylor map of 1783 it has been replaced by Prospect Farm, which is shown in roughly the same location (Illus. 8).

A final word may go to Lord Walter Fitzgerald (1903, 245), who wrote in an article about a prehistoric sculptured stone recovered near Prospect Farm:

'All that I could gather from Murray, the herd on [Prospect] farm, was that the stone was originally built into a castle which formerly stood in a field called "the old town" and that when the ruins were thrown down, the stone was removed to the present dwelling house. The late Mr S. Wilfred Haughton, of Greenbank, Carlow, informed me

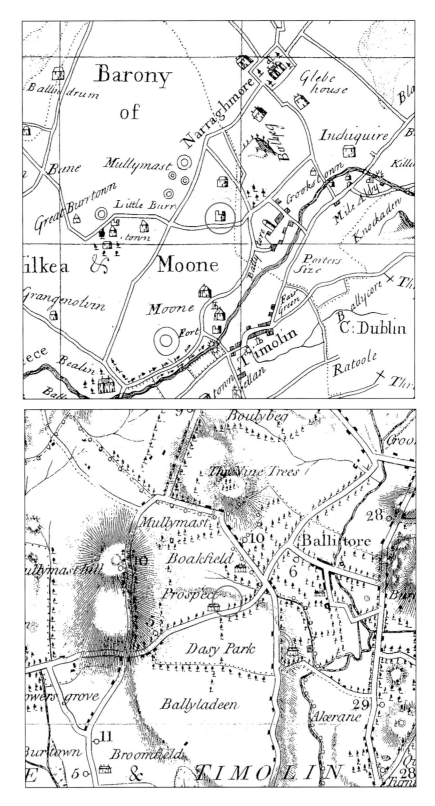

Illus. 8—Noble and Keenan map of 1752 (top); Alexander Taylor map of Kildare, 1783 (bottom), with site location indicated by red circle.

in 1897 (he died recently at a good old age) that his great-grandfather owned the place and demolished the ruins of the Fitzgerald Castle there to build the present dwelling house with the materials.'

Acknowledgements

I would like to thank the NRA, particularly NRA Archaeologist Noel Dunne, for their support for this project; all of the Headland Archaeology Ltd staff who worked on it, particularly those who had to put up with the severe weather conditions of 2007; and Mario Corrigan of the County Kildare Library and Arts Service.

Note

1. NGR 278130, 195837; height 130 m OD; excavation reg. no E2856; ministerial direction no. A021.

15. An 18th-century roadside cottage in Danesfort Demesne, Co. Kilkenny

Richard Jennings and Michelle Delaney

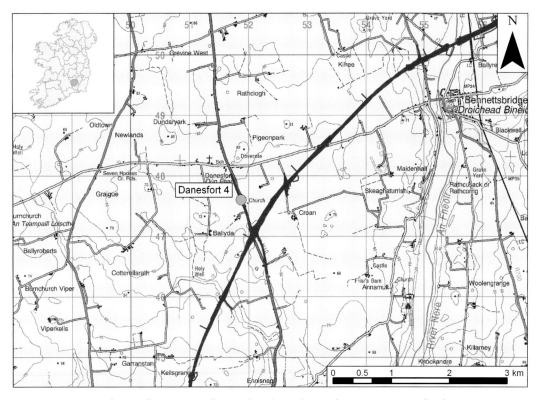

Illus. 1—Location of Danesfort 4, Co. Kilkenny (based on the Ordnance Survey Ireland map).

The study of Ireland's post-1550 archaeology and history has developed considerably in recent years. Traditionally, the archaeology of this period in Ireland was poorly understood and often underrepresented or simply ignored in excavation reports. In recent years, however, there has been a growing understanding of the need to study post-medieval archaeology if we are to understand the profound changes that affected Ireland throughout this period. These cultural, social and economic changes were primarily the result of the transfer of land ownership to new landlords and the settling of that land by immigrants, who came mainly from England and Scotland. The examination of post-medieval archaeology can help us to gain an insight into how the native Irish and Old English, who were descended from the Anglo-Normans, interacted with these new landlords and settlers, and how they adapted as their familiar landscape was profoundly altered.

Archaeological excavations along the route of the N9/N10 Kilcullen–Waterford Scheme: Knocktopher to Powerstown, in the grounds of Danesfort Demesne, Co. Kilkenny, provided an excellent opportunity to examine the evolution of a small portion of a demesne landscape. This paper focuses on the significance of a roadside cottage and its associated domestic/semi-industrial areas found at Danesfort 4 (Illus. 1), less than 200 m from the site of Danesfort House.[1] The intention is to place the site into its historical

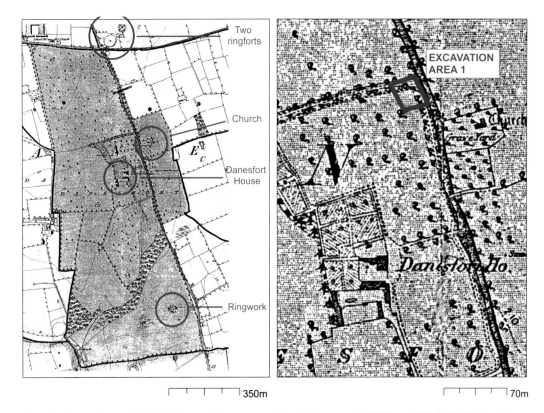

Illus. 2—First edition six-inch Ordnance Survey map (sheet 23, surveyed 1838, published 1840) showing the location of Danesfort demesne and house. The road running north–south and passing between the church and Danesfort House is the Kilkenny–Waterford road, and the road running west–east beside the two ringforts is the Callan–Bennettsbridge road (Ordnance Survey Ireland).

context and to consider its function with the help of maps, documentary sources, paintings and evidence from the few comparable archaeological sites that exist across the country.

The Wemys family of Danesfort

The demesne was part of the former medieval manor of Danesfort and enclosed an area of c. 400 acres (Illus. 2). Historical sources indicate that it was granted to Sir Patrick Wemys (1604–61) by Walter Butler, the 11th Earl of Ormonde. Sir Patrick (knighted c. 1646) was a nobleman from Fife in Scotland and was land commissioner to his cousin, Lady Elizabeth Preston, the future wife of the 1st Duke of Ormonde, when he was granted the land. He married Mary Wheeler, the daughter of the Bishop of Ossory, in 1634 (McEvoy 2006). The life of Sir Patrick coincided with the Catholic Confederate Rebellion, the English Civil War and the period of Cromwellian overlordship, one of the most turbulent times in the history of Ireland (Gillespie 2006). Sir Patrick was a well-known figure who fought as a cavalryman in the Irish Government Army against the Confederate rebellion but who subsequently allied himself to the Parliamentarians led by Oliver Cromwell. He was made a land commissioner in 1653 and an alderman of Kilkenny City in 1656 (McEvoy 2006).

The excavations at Danesfort (Illus. 3) revealed tantalising evidence of Sir Patrick's tenure at the demesne. Two trade tokens (Illus. 4), made by local manufacturers under

Illus. 3—Danesfort 4 under excavation, with the 19th-century farmhouse in the background. Danesfort House was located approximately to the right of the farmhouse, where the vegetation is growing. The avenue of lime trees to the left of the farmhouse leads to the Kilkenny–Waterford road (Richard Jennings).

Illus. 4—One of two trade tokens found at Danesfort 4. Written on the obverse side (left) is 'Francis Barker', and on the reverse side (right) it states 'Of Goran 1656'. The angel depicted is the symbol of the Tanners' Guild (Smith 1852/3) (Aoife McCarthy, Irish Archaeological Consultancy Ltd).

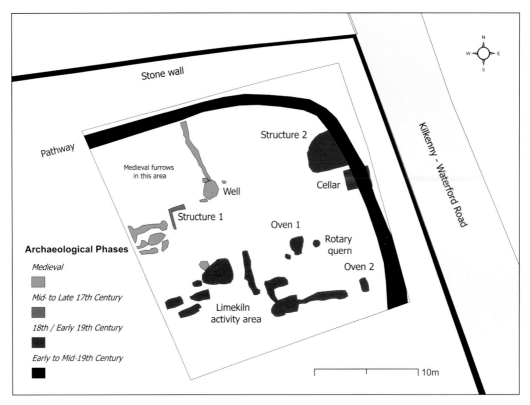

Illus. 5—Plan of the main features excavated at Danesfort 4 (Richard Jennings).

licence from the Cromwellian government in lieu of coinage, and the remains of a small structure (structure 1) were found 30 m west of the roadside cottage (Illus. 5). The remains of the cottage comprised two stone foundations, which would probably have supported timber walls. Seventeenth-century pottery was found on the site, including English Lustre Ware and Frechen stoneware pottery imported from Germany.

A painting of Danesfort House in 1810 provided clues that the estate prospered under the control of Sir Patrick's son, Sir Henry Wemys (1641–1722). The painting shows a large, unfortified structure dating from the 1690s beneath the façades of subsequent 18th-century developments (Illus. 6; McEvoy 2006). The role of the landed estate as a key component of the Irish landscape, where its income was generated through the rental of land to local farmers, continued to develop in the 18th century. Although no known estate records survive, it is probable that the estate experienced a pronounced peak in prosperity during the 1730s and into the 1740s, as occurred elsewhere in New-English-settled Ireland (Reeves-Smyth 1997). The Palladian-style influences evident in the painting by Gibbs of Danesfort House offer an indication of surplus wealth (McEvoy 2006). There is no evidence of how the demesne was set out at this time but it probably had a formal design in keeping with concepts of the Enlightenment such as rationality and control over the natural world (Reeves-Smyth 1997). The demesne would have been at the forefront of economic activity in the locality. Patrick Wemys (1672–1747) succeeded his father Henry as head of the estate and, like his father and grandfather, continued to hold prominent positions in society. He was MP for Gowran in 1703 and 1713–14 and for Kilkenny in 1721–47.

The importance of the Wemys family to Danesfort and Kilkenny continued into the

1750s and 1760s, when Patrick's three sons, Henry, Patrick and James, were each at one point army officers, local MPs and heads of the estate. All three died relatively young, however, and it was James's son, also called James (1755–1820), who inherited the estate in 1763 at the age of seven. He entered the army in 1766 aged just 11 and it was probably not until 1785 that he lived at Danesfort full-time, when genealogical records indicate that he started a family with his wife, Elizabeth Blunden. It is probable that the estate was managed for him between 1763 and 1785.

The roadside cottage

Archaeological evidence points to the construction of the roadside cottage during the mid-18th century. The evidence consisted of a cottage (structure 2) with an adjoining underground storage chamber or cellar (Illus. 5 & 7). It included a cobbled floor surface, 3.74 m by 3.27 m in size, and the remnants of two wall foundations. It is very likely that these were the vestiges of a larger wooden building, probably a cottage, which did not survive. The adjoining cellar contained four stone walls up to seven courses high, with a set of stone steps on its western side leading towards the southern wall of the cottage, where there was evidence for a door. It is probable that the cellar itself had a raised roof or ceiling to protect objects or produce stored inside and to ensure ease of use, as it was excavated to only 1.2 m below ground level. The changes were not just restricted to the construction of a cottage. A 30 m by 10 m area behind the cottage and cellar was stripped of its topsoil and

Illus. 6—The painting of Danesfort House by R Gibbs (from McEvoy 2006).

Illus. 7—A view of the cellar during excavation, from the east (Richard Jennings).

a series of domestic or semi-industrial features were built, including a small limekiln, two ovens, one of which had undergone design modifications, some pits, one of which was stone-lined, and a rotary quern-stone (Illus. 8). A yard area with structural remnants made up of two patches of cobbling and fragmentary stone walls was laid out to the south of this area. The limekiln may have provided the lime mortar used in the construction of the ovens. It was unlikely to have been used for the production of fertiliser for agriculture because of its small size. The main clue linking this development to the mid–late 18th century was the presence of handmade red bricks and the production of lime on the site, both of which became more prevalent in Ireland in the early years of the industrial revolution. An entry in *Finn's Leinster Journal* records the death of a person from lime fumes on the estate in 1774 (cited in Law 2008). Accompanying these features were red burnished wares and clay pipes, find types that fit within this chronological time-frame. This is further reaffirmed by the absence of stoneware and tin-glazed pottery sherds, which are indicators of 17th-century habitation.

The absence of evidence for a structure enclosing the ovens at Danesfort makes it likely that they operated in the open air. Excavated evidence of ovens in Ireland generally comes from urban contexts. Excavations in Waterford between 1986 and 1992 uncovered the remains of at least 20 ovens dating from the 13th to the 17th centuries, the majority of which were open-air structures (Hurley & Sheehan 1997, 274–5). Two open-air ovens excavated near the North Gate Bridge in Cork city date from the mid–late 13th century (Hurley 1997, 39–40). In both cases the ovens were large enough for commercial use (Sherlock 2006, 110). Evidence for mural ovens (ovens constructed in the wall of a building) has also been revealed through archaeological fieldwork. Excavations at

Illus. 8—A mid-excavation view of oven 1, from the west, with the rotary quern-stone in the background (Richard Jennings).

Glanworth Castle, Co. Cork, revealed evidence for two late 16th/early 17th-century ovens (Manning 2000). A late 17th/early 18th-century oven was excavated at O'Dea's Castle in Dysert O'Dea, Co. Clare (Gibson 1997). At Drumlummin, Co. Tipperary, a mural bread oven was uncovered in a mid-17th-century house (Cleary 1987, 124–5). Evidence from England reveals that bake-ovens were often located outside buildings (Hurley & Sheehan 1997, 274).

The presence of bread ovens raises the possibility that the cottage was a bakehouse that sold bread to the inhabitants of Danesfort and to passing traders on the Kilkenny–Waterford Road. Given that the activity took place in full view of the main house, it seems improbable that it occurred when the Wemys family were in full-time residence. There is no indication that the estate was in financial difficulty at this time so it seems unlikely that it was intended as a means to bolster income if the family were in residence. When James was in the army full-time perhaps those managing Danesfort were doing their best to generate additional income for the estate. That said, mid-18th-century demesnes were influenced by the Romantic Movement, in which the idea of having farm cottages close to the main house was not uncommon. It is also worth considering the documentary evidence from the following Calendar of Ormond Deeds (Curtis 1941, 315):

Indenture of May 10, 1582, between Thomas, Earl of Ormond, by Richard Shee of Kilkenny, and Hugh 'alias' Ee Clery of Downefartt, tailor, witnesses that said attorney grants the bakehouse of Downefartt with two crofts belonging to the same, to have and to hold to said Hugh, etc., for 21 years at annual rent of 26s.

The indenture record raises the possibility that a bakehouse was located in the excavated area for perhaps 200 years, although the lack of associated archaeological evidence would suggest that the 1582 bakehouse was in another part of the townland.

If not a bakehouse, the cottage might have been a building to house those responsible for the incoming and outgoing of supplies to the main house from Kilkenny. The ovens were perhaps for the domestic use of those living in the building. A service entry lane to the house is shown on the first edition (1838) Ordnance Survey six-inch map, but it is in the south-east rather than in the north-east, where the cottage was situated. Another possibility is that the cottage housed skilled builders and craftsmen who were responsible for the many renovation works at Danesfort House. It is not clear whether the house underwent renovation during the 20 years that James Wemys was in the army. If there was a link between cottage construction and house renovation, which is plausible given that a skilled workforce was on hand and that bricks used in the construction of the ovens matched those found on a possible wall remnant of the main house (although this may be a secondary build), perhaps the construction of the cottage was associated not with James but with the Palladian-style aspirations of his grandfather Patrick in the 1740s.

Later years

Whatever the reasons for the construction of the roadside cottage, its existence was short-lived as the estate underwent a major transformation towards the end of the century. James took up residence on the demesne, and he and his wife Elizabeth Blunden started a family in 1785. His many years away from Danesfort might explain an advertisement he placed in a Kilkenny newspaper in 1794, stating that Danesfort House and 200 acres were available for rent (*Finn's Leinster Journal*, cited in Law 2008). This did not happen, however, and instead the demesne was transformed into a natural and pastoral landscape. A major element of the change was the construction of a twin-level folly (Sites and Monuments Record No. KK023-080001) on the site of a possible ringwork (KK023-080) (Illus. 9). The architectural components of the folly date from between 1790 and 1810 (www.archaeology.ie, accessed August 2008).

The roadside cottage and its associated features were demolished and replaced with pleasure grounds and a stone path, which formed part of a walkway that followed the perimeter walls of the estate. These walls were also erected at this time. Other aspects of the transformation included the construction to the north of the main house of a walled garden, a glasshouse, an arboretum, which grows to this day, and the avenue of lime trees. A bathhouse was built by the stream in the south-west corner of the demesne. All of these features are depicted on the first edition Ordnance Survey map (Illus. 2).

James was succeeded by his son, Major Henry Wemys, who, in addition to his involvement in the army, continued to manage the estate. As the history of Danesfort entered more recent times, Hubert Butler (1973/4) recalled hearing stories about Henry and his wife Elizabeth as an elderly couple leading 'blameless uneventful lives farming, making jam and taking tea in the summer-house'. Local resident Joseph Ireland recalled hearing stories pertaining to the 1860s about the use of the two-storied turret summer-house, where tea was served downstairs while the gentry shot at deer from upstairs (McEvoy 2006).

Life changed irrevocably for the Wemys of Danesfort in the 1880s when John Otway Wemys, the only child of Henry and Elizabeth, was so overwhelmed with debt owing to

Illus. 9—The 18th/19th-century turret situated on a probable medieval ringwork, from the west (Niall Duffy, AirShots Ltd).

gambling that he fled his creditors by loading up his possessions and moving to London, where he died in 1891. The Wemys estate went into receivership and in 1896 it was put up for sale (McEvoy 2006). The house became derelict and was soon demolished, with the stone ending up as hard core for the Kilkenny–Waterford Road—an inglorious end to more than 250 years of Wemys family influence at Danesfort.

Acknowledgements

We wish to thank NRA Archaeologist Ed Danaher and the NRA for inviting us to contribute to the seminar and publication and for offering the opportunity, in conjunction with Kilkenny City Council, to excavate the site. Thanks also to Irish Archaeological Consultancy Ltd for providing the resources and direction to carry out the dig, in particular Tim Coughlan, Deirdre Walsh, Andrzej Gwozdzik and the rest of the excavation team. Finally, we would like to thank Vicky Ginn of ArchEdit Ireland for proofing an earlier draft of the paper, John Bradley, Colin Rynne, Eoin Grogan, Frank McEvoy and Cóilín Ó Drisceoil for their research input, and Con Barry for his hospitality and for allowing us to explore the remains of the demesne on his land.

Note

1. NGR 251874, 147600; height 63.73 m OD; excavation reg. no. E3539; ministerial direction no. A032.

Appendix 1—Radiocarbon dates from excavated archaeological sites described in these proceedings

Notes

1. Radiocarbon ages are quoted in conventional years BP (before AD 1950), and the errors for these dates are expressed at the one-sigma (68% probability) level of confidence.

2. Calibrated date ranges are equivalent to the probable calendrical age of the sample material and are expressed at one-sigma (68% probability) and two-sigma (95% probability) levels of confidence.

3. Dates obtained from Beta Analytic in Florida (Beta lab code) were calibrated using the IntCal98 calibration dataset (Stuiver et al. 1998) and the Talma & Vogel (1993) calibration programme in the case of Scartbarry 1, Co. Cork, on the M8 Rathcormac/Fermoy Bypass, and using the IntCal04 calibration dataset (Reimer et al. 2004) and the Talma & Vogel (1993) calibration programme in the case of Ballyvass, Co. Kildare, on the N9/N10 Kilcullen–Waterford Scheme: Kilcullen to Carlow, and sites on the N8 Cashel–Mitchelstown Road Improvement Scheme in County Tipperary.

 Dates obtained from Queen's University, Belfast (UB and UBA lab codes), were calibrated using datasets from Stuiver & Reimer (1993) and Reimer et al. (2004) and the CALIB 5.0.2 calibration programme (Stuiver et al. 2005) in the case of Gortore 1, Co. Cork, on the M8 Rathcormac/Fermoy Bypass, and Mitchelstown 1, Co. Cork, on the N8/N73 Mitchelstown Relief Road, Kilcloghans, Co. Galway, on the N17 Tuam Bypass, Sallymount, Co. Limerick, and Killalane and Gortybrigane, Co. Tipperary, on the N7 Nenagh–Limerick High Quality Dual Carriageway, Russellstown and Busherstown, Co. Carlow, on the N9/N10 Kilcullen–Waterford Road Scheme: Prumpelstown to Powerstown, and sites on the N8 Cashel–Mitchelstown Road Improvement Scheme in County Tipperary.

 Dates obtained from the Scottish Universities Environmental Research Centre (SUERC lab code) were calibrated using IntCal04 and the OxCal v.3.10 calibration programme (Bronk Ramsey 2005) in the case of Carrowkeel, Co. Galway, on the N6 Galway to East Ballinasloe PPP Scheme.

4. Radiocarbon dating results from Ballybrowney Lower 1, Co. Cork, on the M8 Rathcormac/Fermoy Bypass, were published previously in O'Sullivan & Stanley 2005, 149. Three radiocarbon dates were returned from Ballinvinny South, Co. Cork, on the N8 Glanmire–Watergrasshill scheme but are considered by the excavator to be spurious and have been discounted.

 Radiocarbon dating results from 40 of the burials at Carrowkeel, Co. Galway, on the N6 Galway to East Ballinasloe PPP Scheme, were published previously in O'Sullivan & Stanley 2007, 155–7.

Lab code	Site	Sample/context	Yrs BP	Calibrated date ranges
Ch. 3 (P Long)—Food for thought: newly discovered cereal-drying kilns from the south-west midlands				
UBA-9928	Killalane bivallate ringfort	Charred rye (*Secale cereale*) grain from basal fill of west side of kiln (possibly drying chamber)	94 ± 24	AD 1696–1917 one sigma AD 1688–1954 two sigma
UBA-9931	Killalane stone-lined, keyhole-shaped kiln	Vetch (*Vicia* sp.) seed from basal deposit at south-west end of flue	1321 ± 24	AD 659–761 one sigma AD 654–768 two sigma
UBA-9934	Sallymount enclosure	Charred hazelnut shell (*Corylus avellana*) from basal fill of kiln	1239 ± 24	AD 692–782 one sigma AD 688–870 two sigma
UBA-9935	Sallymount enclosure	Charred grain of hulled barley (*Hordeum vulgare*) from basal fill of kiln	1320 ± 26	AD 659–762 one sigma AD 653–770 two sigma
UBA-9936	Gortybrigane enclosure	Charred grain of hulled barley (*Hordeum vulgare*) from middle fill of kiln	1546 ± 24	AD 437–557 one sigma AD 430–570 two sigma
UBA-9937	Gortybrigane enclosure	Charred grain of hulled barley (*Hordeum vulgare*) from upper fill of kiln	1605 ± 25	AD 415–532 one sigma AD 408–536 two sigma
UBA-9938	Gortybrigane enclosure	Charred grain of hulled barley (*Hordeum vulgare*) from lower level secondary fill of kiln	1487 ± 24	AD 558–604 one sigma AD 542–633 two sigma
Ch. 6 (T Doyle)—Hair of the dog: evidence of early medieval food production and feasting at Ballyvass, Co. Kildare				
Beta-243988	Ballyvass	Cow bone (femur) from base of ringfort ditch	1280 ± 40	AD 670–770 one sigma AD 660–810 two sigma
Beta-243989	Ballyvass	Charred barley (*Hordeum vulgare*) grain from base of pit	1160 ± 40	AD 810–900 one sigma AD 770–980 two sigma
Ch. 8 (A Kyle et al.)—Excavating a meal: a multidisciplinary approach to early medieval food economy				
UBA-8830	Kilcloghans	Charred wheat (*Triticum dicoccum*) from base of ring-ditch	1187 ± 28	AD 782–883 one sigma AD 727–943 two sigma

Lab code	Site	Sample/context	Yrs BP	Calibrated date ranges
UBA-8831	Kilcloghans	Charred oat (*Avena* sp.) from souterrain fill	1041 ± 44	AD 903–1027 one sigma AD 891–1147 two sigma
UBA-8832	Kilcloghans	Charred hazelnut shell (*Corylus avellana*) from souterrain fill	1162 ± 26	AD 782–941 one sigma AD 778–966 two sigma
UBA-8833	Kilcloghans	Charred barley (*Hordeum vulgare*) grain from pit fill	1154 ± 20	AD 784–950 one sigma AD 780–968 two sigma
UBA-8834	Kilcloghans	Charred barley (*Hordeum vulgare*) grain from souterrain fill	1243 ± 27	AD 690–806 one sigma AD 685–869 two sigma
UBA-8835	Kilcloghans	Oak (*Quercus* sp.) charcoal from ditch fill	1283 ± 36	AD 657–855 one sigma AD 675–855 two sigma
UBA-8836	Kilcloghans	Charred barley (*Hordeum vulgare*) grain from souterrain fill	1201 ± 33	AD 779–872 one sigma AD 694–939 two sigma
SUERC-14057	Carrowkeel	Mouse (*Mus musculus*) bone from enclosure ditch fill	1245 ± 45	AD 680–820 one sigma AD 670–890 two sigma
SUERC-14058	Carrowkeel	Mouse (*Mus musculus*) bone from enclosure ditch fill	1115 ± 35	AD 890–975 one sigma AD 860–1020 two sigma

Ch. 9 (TJ O'Connell & N O'Neill)—A fixed abode: Neolithic houses in County Carlow

Lab code	Site	Sample/context	Yrs BP	Calibrated date ranges
UBA-8447	Busherstown	Unidentifiable burnt bone from fill of pit within house	4640 ± 32	3498–3366 BC one sigma 3517–3358 BC two sigma
UBA-8730	Russellstown	Charred hulled barley (*Hordeum vulgare*) grains from upper fill of enclosure ditch	1027 ± 27	AD 993–1022 one sigma AD 903–1038 two sigma
UBA-8731	Russellstown	Charred hazelnut (*Corylus avellana*) shell from burnt plank wall	4876 ± 30	3694–3641 BC one sigma 3707–3636 BC two sigma
UBA-8734	Russellstown	Charred hazelnut (*Corylus avellana*) shell from packing fill of foundation trench	4946 ± 26	3763–3666 BC one sigma 3776–3657 BC two sigma

Ch. 10 (J Tierney & P Johnston)—No corners! Prehistoric roundhouses on the N8 and N7 in counties Cork, Tipperary and Offaly

Lab code	Site	Sample/context	Yrs BP	Calibrated date ranges
UB-6771	Mitchelstown 1	Hazel (*Corylus* sp.) and alder (*Alnus* sp.) charcoal from fill of internal partition wall slot-trench, structure A	3122 ± 37	1438–1321 BC one sigma 1493–1305 BC two sigma

Lab code	Site	Sample/context	Yrs BP	Calibrated date ranges
UB-6772	Mitchelstown 1	Possible oak (*Quercus* spp) charcoal from stake-hole between structures A & B	3077 ± 39	1407–1313 BC one sigma 1432–1223 BC two sigma
UB-6773	Mitchelstown 1	Willow (*Salix* sp.) and poplar (*Populus* sp.) charcoal from fill of hearth, structure C	3057 ± 38	1392–1273 BC one sigma 1419–1213 BC two sigma
UB-6774	Mitchelstown 1	Hazel (*Corylus* sp.) and alder (*Alnus* sp.) charcoal from fill of structural slot-trench, structure B	3087 ± 37	1412–1315 BC one sigma 1431–1267 BC two sigma

Ch. 11 (M McQuade & C Moriarty)—Hearth and home: Bronze Age structures in south Tipperary

Beta-220333	Knockgraffon, site 129.1	Hazel (*Corylus avellana*) charcoal from post-pipe within post-hole	3200 ± 40	1510–1420 BC one sigma 1530–1400 BC two sigma
UB-7167	Knockgraffon, site 137.1	Hazel (*Corylus avellana*) charcoal from upper fill of circular pit	3114 ± 35	1432–1321 BC one sigma 1489–1297 BC two sigma
UB-7168	Knockgraffon, site 137.1	Hazel (*Corylus avellana*) charcoal from fill of circular pit	3100 ± 34	1422–1317 BC one sigma 1439–1271 BC two sigma
Beta-220336	Knockgraffon, site 137.1	Hazel (*Corylus avellana*), oak (*Quercus*) & ash (*Fraxinus excelsior*) charcoal from fill of post-hole, structure 1	2990 ± 40	1290–1140 BC one sigma 1380–1100 BC two sigma
UB-7172	Cloghabreedy, site 125.4	Hazel (*Corylus avellana*) charcoal from fill of slot-trench, structure A	3290 ± 34	1609–1525 BC one sigma 1666–1494 BC two sigma
UB-7173	Cloghabreedy, site 125.4	Alder (*Alnus glutinosa*) charcoal from fill of post-hole, structure B	3213 ± 35	1506–1441 BC one sigma 1604–1414 BC two sigma
UB-7171	Cloghabreedy, site 125.4	Fruitwood (Pomoideae) charcoal from fill of post-hole	3084 ± 35	1410–1315 BC one sigma 1427–1268 BC two sigma
UB-7205	Killemly, site 203.3	Hazel (*Corylus avellana*) charcoal from fill of pit	3346 ± 33	1688–1541 BC one sigma 1734–1530 BC two sigma

Lab code	Site	Sample/context	Yrs BP	Calibrated date ranges
UB-7206	Killemly, site 203.3	Ash (*Fraxinus*) charcoal from stake-hole, structure A	2918 ± 32	1192–1049 BC one sigma 1256–1012 BC two sigma
UB-7209	Suttonrath, site 206.2	Oak (*Quercus*) charcoal from fill of cooking pit	3238 ± 33	1530–1452 BC one sigma 1607–1436 BC two sigma
UB-7210	Suttonrath, site 206.3	Ash (*Fraxinus*) charcoal from fill of pit	2817 ± 32	1005–926 BC one sigma 1107–1105 BC two sigma
UB-7214	Ballylegan, site 207.1	Cherry (*Prunus avium*) charcoal from slot-trench of circular structure	2805 ± 33	999–919 BC one sigma 1047–893 BC two sigma
UB-7216	Ballylegan, site 207.2	Oak (*Quercus*) charcoal (sapwood) from post-hole, structure B	2861 ± 33	1190–1030 BC one sigma 1253–1007 BC two sigma
UB-7217	Ballylegan, site 207.2	Fruitwood (Pomoideae) charcoal from unenclosed hearth	3318 ± 33	1651–1531 BC one sigma 1686–1519 BC two sigma
UB-7218	Ballylegan, site 207.2	Oak (*Quercus*) charcoal (sapwood) from post-hole, structure A	2861 ± 33	1112–977 BC one sigma 1128–922 BC two sigma
UB-7219	Ballydrehid, site 185.5	Oak (*Quercus*) charcoal from pit within structure B	3097 ± 33	1419–1316 BC one sigma 1435–1271 BC two sigma
UB-7220	Ballydrehid, site 185.5	Willow (*Salix*) charcoal from post-hole of structure A	3119 ± 35	1434–1322 BC one sigma 1492–1304 BC two sigma
Beta-234434	Ballydrehid, site 185.5	Hazel (*Corylus avellana*) charcoal from fill of slot-trench of structure B	3030 ± 40	1330–1260 BC one sigma 1400–1140 BC two sigma
UB-7226	Clonmore North, site 92.3	Hazel (*Corylus avellana*) charcoal from post-hole, structure B	3219 ± 34	1514–1448 BC one sigma 1605–1418 BC two sigma
UB-7227	Clonmore North, site 92.3	Oak (*Quercus*) charcoal from burnt mound of *fulacht fiadh*	3197 ± 34	1496–1498 BC one sigma 1525–1412 BC two sigma
UB-7232	Caherabbey Upper, site 103.1	Ash (*Fraxinus*) charcoal from fill of stake-hole	2789 ± 33	995–903 BC one sigma 1012–843 BC two sigma
UB-7233	Caherabbey Upper, site 104.1	Hazel (*Corylus avellana*) charcoal from fill of pit F23	3026 ± 33	1375–1219 BC one sigma 1396–1133 BC two sigma
UB-7234	Shanballyduff, site 169.1	Apple-type (Pomoideae) charcoal from fill of post-hole	3304±33	1616–1530 BC one sigma 1677–1502 BC two sigma

Lab code	Site	Sample/context	Yrs BP	Calibrated date ranges
UB-7237	Caherabbey Upper, site 185.1–4	Oak (*Quercus*) charcoal from fill of pit	3642 ± 38	2117–1948 BC one sigma 2135–1914 BC two sigma
UB-7377	Cloghabreedy, site 125.3	Fruitwood (Pomoideae) and ash (*Fraxinus*) charcoal from lower fill of circular pit	3762 ± 35	2277–2064 BC one sigma 2289–2041 BC two sigma
UB-7379	Knockgraffon, site 137.3	Seeds (*Hordeum* & *Cerealea*) from fill of pit	3293 ± 34	1611–1526 BC one sigma 1667–1496 BC two sigma
Beta-220337	Knockgraffon, site 137.3	Fruitwood (Pomoideae) charcoal from post-hole, circular structure 1	2810 ± 50	1010–900 BC one sigma 1100–830 BC two sigma
UB-7380	Loughfeedora, site 173.2	Hazel (*Corylus*) & fruitwood (Pomoideae) charcoal from post-hole, D-shaped structure	2830 ± 34	1018–926 BC one sigma 1113–904 BC two sigma
UB-7381	Dogstown, site 151.3	Oak (*Quercus*) charcoal from fill of post-hole, structure 1	3139 ± 34	1452–1388 BC one sigma 1496–1317 BC two sigma
UB-7384	Shanballyduff, site 169a	Hazel (*Corylus avellana*) charcoal from fill of hearth	3375 ± 39	1736–1622 BC one sigma 1753–1532 BC two sigma
UB-7390	Ballylegan, site 207.2	Fruitwood (Pomoideae) charcoal from fill of trough within structure A	2854 ± 33	1108–932 BC one sigma 1122–923 BC two sigma
UB-7392	Ballylegan, site 206.4	Oak (*Quercus*) charcoal from fill of post-hole	2873 ± 48	1125–976 BC one sigma 1211–917 BC two sigma
UB-7507	Dogstown, site 151.3	Hazel (*Corylus avellana*) charcoal from fill of pit, structure 3	3562 ± 36	1963–1786 BC one sigma 2022–1774 BC two sigma
UB-7509	Caherabbey Upper, site 103.1	Fruitwood (Pomoideae) charcoal from fill of well	2761 ± 34	969–843 BC one sigma 997–830 BC two sigma

Ch. 12 (K Hanley)—Reconstructing prehistoric and historic settlement in County Cork

UB-6769	Gortore 1	Oak (*Quercus*) charcoal from fill of house slot-trench	4972 ± 39	3790–3702 BC one sigma 3928–3655 BC two sigma
Beta-201080	Scartbarry 1	Alder (*Alnus*) charcoal from heat-shattered stone in trough	3470 ± 60	1880–1700 BC one sigma 1940–1630 BC two sigma
Beta-201081	Scartbarry 1	Hazel (*Corylus avellana*) charcoal from fill of pit	3150 ± 60	1490–1390 BC one sigma 1520–1290 BC two sigma

Lab code	Site	Sample/context	Yrs BP	Calibrated date ranges
Beta-201082	Scartbarry 1	Oak (*Quercus*) charcoal from fill of slot-trench enclosing trough	3030 ± 80	1400–1140 BC one sigma 1440–1020 BC two sigma
Beta-201083	Scartbarry 1	Hazel (*Corylus avellana*) charcoal from primary fill of stone-lined trough	3160 ± 100	1520–1320 BC one sigma 1650–1190 BC two sigma
Beta-201084	Scartbarry 1	Oak (*Quercus*) charcoal from fill of second *fulacht fiadh* trough in area B	2970 ± 90	1400–1140 BC one sigma 1440–1020 BC two sigma

References

Allingham, H 1896 'Wooden objects found in peat bogs, supposed to have been otter traps', *Proceedings of the Royal Society of Antiquaries of Ireland*, Vol. 26, 379–82.

Bailey, D W 1996 'The life, times and works of House 59, Tell Ovcharovo, Bulgaria', *in* T Darvill & J Thomas (eds), *Neolithic Houses in North-west Europe and Beyond*, 143–56. Oxbow Monograph Series 57. Oxbow, Oxford.

Bankoff, H A & Winter, F 1979 'A house-burning in Serbia: what do burned remains tell an archaeologist?', *Archaeology,* Vol. 32, No. 5, 8–14.

Barratt, P, Whitehouse, N J, Schulting, R, McLaughlin, R, McClatchie, M, Reimer, P J & Bogaard, A (in prep.) 'Testing Time: an approach to analysing radiocarbon dates as data from Irish Mesolithic, Neolithic, and Bronze Age archaeological sites', *Journal of Archaeological Science*.

Bartlett, A 2002 *N9/N10 Northern Section, report on archaeogeophysical survey*. Unpublished report by Bartlett–Clark Consultancy for Kildare County Council.

Bartlett, A 2005 *Archaeological Geophysical Survey on the Route of the N18 Gort to Crusheen National Road Scheme*. Unpublished report by Bartlett–Clark Consultancy for Galway County Council.

Bayley, D 2006 *Kilcullen to Waterford Scheme: Kilcullen to Powerstown archaeological services contract. Contract 1, Kilcullen to Mullamast, archaeology assessment N9/N10*. Unpublished report by Irish Archaeological Consultancy Ltd for Kildare County Council.

Bell, J 1984 'A contribution to the study of cultivation ridges in Ireland', *Journal of the Royal Society of Antiquaries of Ireland*, Vol. 114, 80–97.

Bell, J 2008 *A History of Irish Farming: 1750–1950*. Four Courts Press, Dublin.

Bell, J & Watson, M 1986 *Irish Farming 1750–1900: implements and techniques*. John Donaldson, Edinburgh.

Bell, R 1804 *A Description of the Conditions and Manners as well as the Moral and Political Character, Education etc. of the Peasantry of Ireland such as They Were between the Years 1780 and 1790*. London.

Bogaard, A, Heaton, T H E, Poulton, P & Merbach, I 2007 'The impact of manuring on nitrogen isotope ratios in cereals: archaeological implications for reconstruction of diet and crop management practices', *Journal of Archaeological Science*, Vol. 34, No. 3, 335–43.

Bonsall, J & Gimson, H 2004a *Archaeological geophysical survey of the route of the N6 Ballinasloe to Athlone national road scheme*. Unpublished report by Earthsound Archaeological Geophysics for Galway County Council.

Bonsall, J & Gimson, H 2004b 'Geophysical perspectives in archaeology', *Archaeology Ireland*, Vol. 18, No. 3, 22–5.

Bonsall, J & Gimson, H 2006a *Archaeological geophysical survey of the route of the N6 Galway City Outer Bypass*. Unpublished report by Earthsound Archaeological Geophysics for Galway County Council.

Bonsall, J & Gimson, H 2006b *Archaeological geophysical survey of the route of the M17 Galway to Tuam national road scheme*. Unpublished report by Earthsound Archaeological Geophysics for Galway County Council.

Bronk Ramsey, C 2005 *OxCal Program v.3.10* (http://www.rlaha.ox.ac.uk/O/oxcal.php).

Brooks, E St J 1931−2 'The family of Marisco: part 2', *Journal of the Royal Society of Antiquaries of Ireland*, Vol. 61, Part 2, 89−112.

Brooks, E St J 1952a 'The de Ridelisfords: part 1', *Journal of the Royal Society of Antiquaries of Ireland*, Vol. 82, Part 1, 45–62.

Brooks, E St J 1952b 'The de Ridelisfords: part 2', *Journal of the Royal Society of Antiquaries of Ireland*, Vol. 81, Part 2, 115–39.

Brossler, A, Early, E & Allen, C 2004 *Green Park (Reading Business Park), Phase 2 Excavations 1995: Neolithic and Bronze Age Sites*. Thames Valley Landscape Monographs 19. Oxford Archaeology, Oxford.

Brown, P 2003 *Man Walks into a Pub*. Macmillan, London.

Brück, J 1999 'Houses, lifecycles and deposition on Middle Bronze Age settlements in Southern England', *Proceedings of the Prehistoric Society*, Vol. 65, 145–66.

Butler, H 1973/4 'Kilkenny in the days of the Dukes', *Journal of the Butler Society*, Vol. 1, No. 5, 339–46.

Channing, J & Randolph-Quinney, P 2006 'Death, decay and reconstruction: the archaeology of Ballykilmore cemetery, County Westmeath', *in* J O'Sullivan & M Stanley (eds), *Settlement, Industry and Ritual*, 115–28. Archaeology and the National Roads Authority Monograph Series No. 3. National Roads Authority, Dublin.

Church, A J & Brodribb, W J (trans.) 1877 *The Agricola and the Germania*. Macmillan, London.

Civil, M 1964 'A Hymn to the Beer Goddess and a Drinking Song', *in* R D Briggs & J A Brinkman (eds), *Studies Presented to A. Leo Oppenheim, June 7, 1964*, 67–89. The Oriental Institute of the University of Chicago, Chicago.

Clark, A 1990 [2nd edn, 1996] *Seeing Beneath the Soil: prospecting methods in archaeology*. Batsford, London.

Clarke, L & Carlin, N 2008 'Living with the dead at Johnstown 1: an enclosed burial, settlement and industrial site', *in* N Carlin, L Clarke & F Walsh, *The Archaeology of Life and Death in the Boyne Floodplain: the linear landscape of the M4*, 55–85. NRA Scheme Monographs 2. National Roads Authority, Dublin.

Clarkson, L & Crawford, M 2001 *Feast and Famine: food and nutrition in Ireland, 1500–1920*. Oxford University Press.

Cleary, R M 1987 'Drumlummin, Co. Tipperary', *in* R M Cleary, M F Hurley & E A Twohig (eds), *Archaeological Excavations on the Cork–Dublin Gas Pipeline (1981–82)*, 116–45. Cork Archaeological Studies No. 1. Department of Archaeology, University College Cork.

Cleary, R M 1995 'Later Bronze Age settlement and prehistoric burials, Lough Gur, Co. Limerick', *Proceedings of the Royal Irish Academy*, Vol. 95C, 1–92.

Clinton, M 2001 *The Souterrains of Ireland*. Wordwell, Bray.

Conran, S 2008 'New roads, new discoveries', *Seanda*, No. 3, 31–2.

Conway, M 2000 *Director's First Findings from Excavations at Cabinteely*. Margaret Gowen & Co. Ltd Transactions 1. Margaret Gowen & Co. Ltd, Dublin.

Cooney, G 2000 *Landscapes of Neolithic Ireland*. Routledge, London.

Cooney, G 2003 'Rooted or routed? Landscapes of Neolithic settlement in Ireland', *in* I Armit, E Murphy, E Nelis & D Simpson (eds), *Neolithic Settlement in Ireland and Western Britain*, 47–55. Oxbow Books, Oxford.

Cooney, G & Grogan, E 1999 *Irish Prehistory: a social perspective* (2nd edn). Wordwell, Bray.

Cotter, C 1993 'Western Stone Fort Project: interim report', *Discovery Programme Reports*, No. 1, 1–19. Royal Irish Academy/Discovery Programme, Dublin.

Cotter, E 2005 'Bronze Age Ballybrowney, County Cork', *in* J O'Sullivan & M Stanley (eds), *Recent Archaeological Discoveries on National Road Schemes 2004*, 37–43. Archaeology and the National Roads Authority Monograph Series No. 2. National Roads Authority, Dublin.

Curtis, E (ed.) 1941 *Calendar of Ormond Deeds, Volume V, 1547–1584*. The Stationery Office for the Irish Manuscripts Commission, Dublin.

D'Alton, J 1838 *The History of the County of Dublin*. R Gattsberry, Dublin.

Danaher, E 2007 *Monumental Beginnings: the archaeology of the N4 Sligo Inner Relief Road*. NRA Scheme Monographs 1. National Roads Authority, Dublin.

Devitt, M 1916 'The Barony of Okethy', *Journal of the County Kildare Archaeological Society*, Vol. 8, No. 4, 276–301.

Dineley, M 2004 *Barley, Malt and Ale in the Neolithic*. Archaeopress, Oxford.

Doody, M G 1987 'Ballyveelish, Co. Tipperary', *in* R M Cleary, M F Hurley & E A Twohig (eds), *Archaeological Excavations on the Cork–Dublin Gas Pipeline (1981–82)*, 9–35. Cork Archaeological Studies No. 1. Department of Archaeology, University College Cork.

Doody, M 2000 'Bronze Age houses in Ireland', *in* A Desmond, G Johnson, M McCarthy et al. (eds), *New Agendas in Irish Prehistory: papers in commemoration of Liz Anderson*, 135–59. Wordwell, Bray.

Doody, M 2007 *Excavations at Curraghatoor, Co. Tipperary*. UCC Department of Archaeology, Archaeological Monograph. University College Cork.

Drewett, P 1982 'Late Bronze Age Downland economy and excavations at Black Patch, East Sussex', *Proceedings of the Prehistoric Society*, Vol. 48, 321–400.

Dudley, R 2004 'Ethanol, fruit ripening, and the historical origins of human alcoholism in primate frugivory', *Integrative and Comparative Biology*, Vol. 44, No. 4, 315–23.

Dutton, H 1824 *A Statistical and Agricultural Survey of the County of Galway*. Royal Dublin Society, Dublin.

Edwards, N 1990 *The Archaeology of Early Medieval Ireland*. Routledge, London.

Ellison, A 1981 'Towards a socioeconomic model for the Middle Bronze Age in Southern England', *in* I Hodder, G Isaac & N Hammond (eds), *Pattern of the Past: studies in honour of David Clarke*, 413–38. Cambridge University Press, Cambridge.

Evans, E E 1957 [2nd edn, 1967] *Irish Folkways*. Routledge & Kegan Paul, London.

Faegri, K & Iverson, J 1975 *Textbook of Pollen Analysis*. Blackwell, Oxford.

Fahy, E M 1959 'A recumbent stone circle at Drombeg, Co. Cork', *Journal of the Cork Historical and Archaeological Society*, Vol. 64, 1–27.

Fairweather, A D & Ralston, I B M 1993 'The Neolithic timber hall at Balbridie, Grampian Region, Scotland: the building, the date, the plant macrofossils', *Antiquity*, Vol. 67, 313–23.

Farrelly, J & O'Brien, C (comp.) 2002 *Archaeological Inventory of Tipperary Vol. 1—North Tipperary*. The Stationery Office, Dublin.

FitzGerald, M 2006 'Archaeological discoveries on a new section of the N2 in counties Meath and Dublin', *in* J O'Sullivan & M Stanley (eds), *Settlement, Industry and Ritual*, 29–42. Archaeology and the National Roads Authority Monograph Series No. 3. National Roads Authority, Dublin.

Fitzgerald, W 1895 'Mullaghmast: its history and traditions', *Journal of the County Kildare Archaeological Society*, Vol. 1, No. 6, 379–90.

Fitzgerald, W 1903 'Miscellanea: the Mullaghmast Sculptured Boulder', *Journal of the*

County Kildare Archaeological Society, Vol. 4, No. 3, 245–8.

Fitzpatrick, A P, Butterworth, C A & Grove, J 1999 *Prehistoric and Roman Sites in East Devon: the A30 Honiton to Exeter Improvement DBFO Scheme, 1996–9*. Trust for Wessex Archaeology, Salisbury.

Frame, R 1996 'The defence of the English Lordship, 1250–1450', *in* T Bartlett & K Jeffery (eds), *A Military History of Ireland*, 76–98. Cambridge University Press, Cambridge.

Franklin, J 2008 *N6 Galway to Ballinasloe Carrowkeel Finds Report*. Unpublished report prepared for Headland Archaeology Ltd.

Gailey, A 1982 *Spade Making in Ireland*. Ulster Folk & Transport Museum, Holywood, Co. Down.

Geber, J, Halwas, S & O'Donnell, L 2009 'The environmental and faunal evidence', *in* M McQuade, B Molloy & C Moriarty, *In the Shadow of the Galtees: archaeological excavations along the N8 Cashel to Mitchelstown Road Scheme*, 239–84. NRA Scheme Monographs 4. National Roads Authority, Dublin.

Gent, H 1983 'Centralized storage in later prehistoric Britain', *Proceedings of the Prehistoric Society*, Vol. 49, 243–67.

Gerriets, M 1983 'Economy and society: clientship according to the Irish laws', *Cambridge Medieval Celtic Studies*, Vol. 6, 43–61.

Gibson, A M 2002 *Prehistoric Pottery in Britain and Ireland*. Tempus, Stroud.

Gibson, D B 1997 '1996 Excavations at O'Dea's Castle, Dysert O'Dea, County Clare: Summary Report', *The Other Clare*, Vol. 21, 47–8.

Gillespie, R 2006 *Seventeenth-century Ireland: making Ireland modern*. Gill & Macmillan, Dublin.

Gowen, M 1988 'House site', *in* M Gowen (ed.), *Three Irish Gas Pipelines: new archaeological evidence in Munster*, 26–43. Wordwell, Dublin.

Gowen, M & Halpin, E 1992 'A Neolithic House at Newtown', *Archaeology Ireland*, Vol. 6, No. 2, 25–7.

Gowen, M & Tarbett, C 1988 'A third season at Tankardstown', *Archaeology Ireland*, Vol. 2, No. 4, 156.

Graham-Smith, M D 1923 'On the methods employed in using the so-called otter or beaver traps', *Proceedings of the Royal Society of Antiquaries of Scotland*, Vol. 57, 48–54.

Griffiths, I 2007 *Beer and Cider in Ireland*. Liberties Press, Dublin.

Groenman van Waateringe, W 1984 'Appendix 2: Pollen and seed analyses', *in* G Eogan (ed.), *Excavations at Knowth 1: smaller passage tombs, Neolithic occupation and Beaker activity*, 325–9. Royal Irish Academy, Dublin.

Grogan, E 2002 'Neolithic houses in Ireland: a broader perspective', *Antiquity*, Vol. 76, 517–25.

Grogan, E 2004 'The implications of Irish Neolithic houses', *in* I Shepherd & G Barclay (eds), *Scotland in Ancient Europe*, 103–14. Society of Antiquaries of Scotland, Edinburgh.

Grogan, E & Roche, H 2009 'The prehistoric pottery', *in* M McQuade, B Molloy & C Moriarty, *In the Shadow of the Galtees: archaeological excavations along the N8 Cashel to Mitchelstown Road Scheme*, 286–312. NRA Scheme Monographs 4. National Roads Authority, Dublin.

Guilbert, G 1982 'Post-ring symmetry in roundhouses at Moel y Gaer and some other sites in prehistoric Britain', *in* P J Drury (ed.), *Structural Reconstruction: approaches to the interpretation of excavated remains of buildings*, 67–86. British Archaeological Reports, British Series 110. Oxford.

Gwynn, E J (ed. & trans.) 1905 'The three drinking horns of Cormac úa Cuinn (from the Liber Flavus Fergusiorum)', *Ériu*, Vol. 2, 186–8.

Hammond, P 1993 *Food and Feast in Medieval England*. Sutton Publishing, Stroud.

Hanley, K 2008 'Digital evolution: 3D-animated reconstructions from County Cork', *Seanda*, No. 3, 62–3.

Hegarty, L 2005 'A saddle quern discovered on Site 43, in Ballyduff East, on the route of the N25 Waterford City Bypass', *in* J O'Sullivan & M Stanley (eds), *Recent Archaeological Discoveries on National Road Schemes 2004*, 45–50. Archaeology and the National Roads Authority Monograph Series No. 2. National Roads Authority, Dublin.

Hillman, G C 1981 'Reconstructing crop husbandry practices from charred remains of crops', *in* R Mercer (ed.), *Farming Practice in British Prehistory*, 123–62. Edinburgh University Press, Edinburgh.

Hornsey, I S 2003 *A History of Beer and Brewing*. RSC Paperbacks, Cambridge.

Hull, G 2007 'Knockdomny', *in* E Grogan, L O'Donnell & P Johnston, *The Bronze Age Landscapes of the Pipeline to the West: an integrated archaeological and environmental assessment*, 347–9. Wordwell, Bray.

Hurley, M F 1997 *Excavations at the North Gate, Cork, 1994*. Cork Corporation, Cork.

Hurley, M F & Sheehan, C M 1997 'Ovens and kilns', *in* M F Hurley, O M B Scully, R M Cleary & S W J McCutcheon (eds), *Late Viking Age and Medieval Waterford: excavations 1986–1992*, 273–7. Waterford Corporation, Waterford.

Johnston, P 2003 'Analysis of the plant remains', *in* R Tobin, *Corbally 2001/2002 (Licence no. 01E0299), stratigraphic report; kilns and associated features.* Unpublished report for Margaret Gowen and Co. Ltd.

Jones, G, Charles, C, Bogaard, A, Hodgson, J G & Palmer, C 2004 'The functional ecology of present-day arable weed floras and its applicability for the identification of past crop husbandry', *Vegetation History and Archaeobotany*, Vol. 14, 493–504.

Jones, G & Rowley-Conwy, P 2007 'On the importance of cereal cultivation in the British Neolithic', *in* S Colledge & J Conolly (eds), *The Origins and Spread of Domestic Plants in Southwest Asia and Europe*, 391–419. Left Coast Press, Walnut Creek, California.

Jones, M 2007 *Feast: why humans share food*. Oxford University Press, Oxford.

Jones, M K 1985 'Archaeobotany beyond subsistence reconstruction', *in* G W Barker & C Gamble (eds), *Beyond Domestication in Prehistoric Europe*, 107–28. Academic Press, New York and London.

Kelly, F 2000 *Early Irish Farming*. Early Irish Law Series 4. Dublin Institute for Advanced Studies, Dublin.

Kelly, F 2005 *A Guide to Early Irish Law* (2nd edn). Dublin Institute for Advanced Studies, Dublin.

Kenward, H K & Allison, E P 1994 'A preliminary view of the insect assemblages from the Early Christian rath site at Deer Park Farms, Northern Ireland', *in* J Rackham (ed.), *Environment and Economy in Anglo-Saxon England*, 89–103. CBA Research Report 89. Council for British Archaeology, York.

Knox, H T 1907 'Notes on gig-mills and drying kilns near Ballyhaunis, Co. Mayo', *Proceedings of the Royal Irish Academy*, Vol. 26C, 265–74.

Krahn, H 2005 *Archaeological geophysical survey of the route of the N18 Oranmore to Gort national road scheme.* Unpublished report by Minerex Geophysics Ltd for Galway County Council.

Kyle, A 2007 *Souterrain Ware: petrology, provenance and production.* Unpublished Master's thesis, University of Southampton.

Kyle, A 2008 'The Metal Finds', *in* L McKinstry, *N17 Tuam Bypass, Co. Galway. Final report on archaeological excavation of a univallate ringfort and souterrain at Kilcloghans, Co. Galway.* Unpublished excavation report, Headland Archaeology Ltd.

Law, E 2008 *Kilkenny History Miscellaneous Houses* (http://homepage.eircom.net/ ~lawekk/HSESD.HTM, accessed December 2008).

Logan, E 2007 'Uncovering Carlow's oldest farmstead', *Seanda*, No. 2, 67–8.

Lucas, A T 1970 'Paring and burning in Ireland: a preliminary survey', *in* R A Gailey & A Fenton (eds), *The Spade in Northern and Atlantic Europe*, 99–147. Ulster Folk Museum with Institute of Irish Studies, Queen's University, Belfast.

McClatchie, M (forthcoming) 'Cultivating societies: assessing the evidence for cereal remains in Neolithic Ireland', *in* R Schulting, N Whitehouse & M McClatchie (eds), *Living Landscapes: exploring Neolithic Ireland and its wider context.* Archaeopress, Oxford.

McCormick, F 1987 *Stockrearing in Early Christian Ireland.* Unpublished Ph.D thesis, Queen's University, Belfast.

McCormick, F 2002 'The distribution of meat in a hierarchical society: the Irish evidence', *in* P Miracle & N Milner (eds), *Consuming Passions and Patterns of Consumption*, 25–31. McDonald Institute Monographs, Cambridge.

McCormick, F & Murray, E 2007 *Knowth and the Zooarchaeology of Early Christian Ireland.* Excavations at Knowth 3. Royal Irish Academy, Dublin.

MacDonagh, M 2005 'Valley bottom and hilltop: 6,000 years of settlement along the route of the N4 Sligo Inner Relief Road', *in* J O'Sullivan & M Stanley (eds), *Recent Archaeological Discoveries on National Road Schemes 2004*, 9–23. Archaeology and the National Roads Authority Monograph Series No. 2. National Roads Authority, Dublin.

McEvoy, F 2006 'The Wemyss family of Danesfort, Co. Kilkenny', *Old Kilkenny Review*, Vol. 58, 127–38.

McEvoy, J 1802 *Statistical Survey of County Tyrone.* Royal Dublin Society, Dublin.

McGovern, P E, Zhang, J, Tang, J et al. 2004 'Fermented beverages of pre- and proto-historic China', *Proceedings of the National Academy of Sciences*, Vol. 101, 17593–8.

MacGregor, A 1985 *Bone, Antler, Ivory and Horn from Anglo-Scandinavian and Medieval York.* York Archaeological Trust, York.

McKinstry, L 2008 'Everyday life in early medieval Galway', *Seanda*, No. 3, 12.

McLaren, F, Monk, M & Sexton, R 2004 'Burning the biscuit: evidence from the Lisleagh excavations reveals new secrets twenty years on!', *Archaeology Ireland,* Vol. 18, No. 3, 18–20.

McQuade, M, Molloy, B & Moriarty, C 2009 *In the Shadow of the Galtees: archaeological excavations along the N8 Cashel to Mitchelstown Road Scheme.* NRA Scheme Monographs 4. National Roads Authority, Dublin.

McSparron, C 2008 'Have you no homes to go to?', *Archaeology Ireland,* Vol. 22, No. 3, 18–21.

MacSween, A 2008 *Carlow Bypass: report on the pottery from Busherstown (E2581).* Unpublished client report for Headland Archaeology Ltd.

Manning, C 2000 *Glanworth: a medieval castle, friary and town in County Cork.* Archaeology Ireland Heritage Guide No. 9. Wordwell, Bray.

Michel, R H, McGovern, P E & Badler, V R 1992 'Chemical evidence for ancient beer', *Nature*, Vol. 360, 24.

Mitchell, F 1945 'The relative ages of archaeological objects recently found in bogs in Ireland', *Proceedings of the Royal Irish Academy*, Vol. 100C, 1–19.

Mitchell, F & Ryan, M 1997 *Reading the Irish Landscape* (3rd edn). Town House, Dublin.

Moffet, L 2006 'The archaeology of medieval plant foods', *in* C M Woolgar, D Serjeantson & T Waldren (eds), *Food in Medieval England: diet and nutrition*, 44–55. Oxford University Press, Oxford.

Monk, M 1988 'Appendix 3. Archaeobotanical study of samples from pipeline sites', *in* M Gowen (ed.), *Three Irish Gas Pipelines: new archaeological evidence in Munster*, 185–91. Wordwell, Dublin.

Monk, M 1991 'The archaeobotanical evidence for field crop plants in early historic Ireland', *in* J M Renfrew (ed.), *New Light on Early Farming: recent developments in palaeoethnobotany*, 315–28. Edinburgh University Press, Edinburgh.

Monk, M A & Kelleher, E 2005 'An assessment of the archaeological evidence for Irish corn-drying kilns in the light of the results of archaeological experiments and archaeobotanical studies', *Journal of Irish Archaeology*, Vol. 14, 77–114.

Monsen, E (ed.) 1932 *Heimskringla or the Lives of the Norse Kings by Snorre Sturlason*. Cambridge University Press, Cambridge.

Moore, C 2007 'Right on track at Edercloon', *Seanda*, No. 2, 20–1.

Moore, C 2008 'Old routes to new research: the Edercloon wetland excavations in County Longford', *in* J O'Sullivan & M Stanley (eds), *Roads, Rediscovery and Research*, 1–12. Archaeology and the National Roads Authority Monograph Series No. 5. National Roads Authority, Dublin.

Morrin, J (ed.) 1861 *Calendar of the Patent and Close Rolls of Chancery in Ireland, Vol. 1.* Her Majesty's Stationery Office, Dublin.

Moszynski, K 1929 *Kultura Ludowa Stowian.* Polska Akademia Umiejetnosci, Krakow.

Mulally, E (ed.) 2002 *The Deeds of the Normans in Ireland (La Geste des Engleis en Yrlande).* Four Courts Press, Dublin.

Munro, R & Gillespie, P 1919 'Further notes on ancient wooden traps—the so-called otter and beaver traps', *Proceedings of the Royal Society of Antiquaries of Scotland*, Vol. 53, 162–5.

Murphy, D & Rathbone, S 2006 'Excavation of an early medieval vertical watermill at Killoteran, County Waterford', *in* J O'Sullivan & M Stanley (eds), *Settlement, Industry and Ritual*, 19–28. Archaeology and the National Roads Authority Monograph Series No. 3. National Roads Authority, Dublin.

Murray, E & McCormick, F 2005 'Environmental analysis and the food supply', *in* J W Marshall & C Walsh, *Illaunloughan Island: an early medieval monastery in County Kerry*, 67–80. Wordwell, Bray.

Nelson, M 2005 *The Barbarian's Beverage: a history of beer in ancient Europe.* Routledge, New York.

Noble, J & Keenan, J 1752 *Map of 1752.* Local Studies, Genealogy and Archives Department, Kildare Library and Arts Service, Newbridge.

O'Brien, E 1992 'Pagan and Christian burial in Ireland during the first millennium AD: continuity and change', *in* N Edwards & A Lane (eds), *The Early Church in Wales and the West: recent work in Early Christian archaeology, history and placenames*, 130–7. Oxbow Monograph 16. Oxbow, Oxford.

O'Byrne, E 2003 *War, Politics and the Irish of Leinster, 1156–1606.* Four Courts Press,

Dublin.

O'Connor, T P 1991 *Bones from 46–54 Fishergate*. The Archaeology of York: the animal bones 15/4. Council for British Archaeology, York.

O'Connor, T P 2003 *The Analysis of Urban Animal Bone Assemblages: a handbook for archaeologists*. The Archaeology of York: principles and methods 19/2. Council for British Archaeology, York.

Ó Corráin, D 2005 'Ireland c. 800: aspects of society', *in* D Ó Cróinín (ed.), *A New History of Ireland I: prehistoric and early Ireland*, 549–607. Oxford University Press, Oxford.

Ó Cróinín, D 1995 *Early Medieval Ireland 400–1200*. Longman, Pearson Education Ltd, Harlow.

Ó Danachair, C 1970 'The use of the spade in Ireland', *in* R A Gailey & A Fenton (eds), *The Spade in Northern and Atlantic Europe*, 49–56. Ulster Folk Museum with Institute of Irish Studies, Queen's University, Belfast.

Ó Floinn, R 1991 'Later medieval decorative arts', *in* M Ryan (ed.), *Irish Archaeology Illustrated*, 194–5, 216. Country House, Dublin.

O'Kelly, M J 1954 'Excavations and experiments in ancient Irish cooking places', *Journal of the Royal Society of Antiquaries of Ireland*, Vol. 84, 105–55.

O'Meara, J J (ed. & trans.) 1982 *Giraldus Cambrensis: the history and topography of Ireland*. Penguin Books, London.

Ó Néill, J 2004 'Lapidibus in igne calefactis coquebatur: the historical burnt mound tradition', *Journal of Irish Archaeology,* Vols 12 & 13, 79–85.

O'Neill, T 2007 'The hidden past of Parknahown, Co. Laois', *in* J O'Sullivan & M Stanley (eds), *New Routes to the Past*, 133–9. Archaeology and the National Roads Authority Monograph Series No. 4. National Roads Authority, Dublin.

Ó Nualláin, S 1972 'A Neolithic house at Ballyglass near Ballycastle, Co. Mayo', *Journal of the Royal Society of Antiquaries of Ireland,* Vol. 106, 92–117.

Ó Nualláin, S 1984 'A survey of stone circles in Cork and Kerry', *Proceedings of the Royal Irish Academy*, Vol. 84C, 1–77.

Ó Ríordáin, S P 1943 'A built-in oven near Cove, Co. Cork', *Journal of the Cork Historical and Archaeological Society*, Vol. 48, 154–5.

Orpen, G H O 2005 [reprint] *Ireland under the Normans, 1169–1333*. Four Courts Press, Dublin.

O'Sullivan, J 2007a 'Search and discovery on an east Galway road scheme', *Seanda*, No. 2, 22–5.

O'Sullivan, J 2007b 'The quiet landscape: archaeological discoveries on a road scheme in east Galway', *in* J O'Sullivan & M Stanley (eds), *New Routes to the Past*, 81–100. Archaeology and the National Roads Authority Monograph Series No. 4. National Roads Authority, Dublin.

O'Sullivan, J & Stanley, M (eds) 2005 'Appendix 1—Radiocarbon dates from excavated archaeological sites described in these proceedings', *Recent Archaeological Discoveries on National Road Schemes 2004*, 147–53. Archaeology and the National Roads Authority Monograph Series No. 2. National Roads Authority, Dublin.

O'Sullivan, J & Stanley, M (eds) 2007 'Appendix 1—Radiocarbon dates from excavated archaeological sites described in these proceedings', *in* J O'Sullivan & M Stanley (eds), *New Routes to the Past*, 153–61. Archaeology and the National Roads Authority Monograph Series No. 4. National Roads Authority, Dublin.

O'Sullivan, J, Tierney, J & Wilkins, B (forthcoming) 'Rural vernacular industry in early modern Galway: recent excavations on national road schemes', *in* S Bourke (ed.), *Archaeology of Irish Industry.*

Otway-Ruthven, A J 1980 *A History of Medieval Ireland* (2nd edn). Ernest Benn, London.

Prestwich, M 2005 *Plantagenet England, 1225−1360.* Oxford University Press, Oxford.

Purcell, A 2002 'Excavation of three Neolithic houses at Corbally, Kilcullen, Co. Kildare', *Journal of Irish Archaeology,* Vol. 11, 31–75.

Quinn, B & Moore, D 2007 'Ale brewing and *fulachta fiadh*', *Archaeology Ireland,* Vol. 21, No. 3, 8–17.

Rackham, D J 2004 'Physical remains of medieval horses', *in* J Clark (ed.), *The Medieval Horse and its Equipment c. 1150–c. 1450,* 19–22. Medieval Finds from Excavations in London: 5. Museum of London, London.

Reeves-Smyth, T 1997 'Demesnes', *in* F H A Aalen, K Whelan & M Stout (eds), *Atlas of the Irish Rural Landscape,* 197–205. Cork University Press, Cork.

Reimer, P J, Baillie, M G L, Bard, E et al. 2004 'IntCal04 terrestrial radiocarbon age calibration, 0–26 cal kyr BP', *Radiocarbon,* Vol. 46, No. 3, 1029–58.

Rice, P 1987 *Pottery Analysis: a sourcebook.* University of Chicago Press, Chicago and London.

Roseveare, M & Roseveare, A 2003 *Archaeological geophysical survey on the route of the N6 Loughrea Bypass.* Unpublished report by ArchaeoPhysica Ltd for Galway County Council.

Roseveare, M & Roseveare, A 2004a *Archaeological geophysical survey on the route of the N6 Galway to Ballinsloe national road scheme.* Unpublished report by ArchaeoPhysica Ltd for Galway County Council.

Roseveare, M & Roseveare, A 2004b *Archaeological geophysical survey on the route of the N17 Castletown Realignment.* Unpublished report by ArchaeoPhysica Ltd for Galway County Council.

Roseveare, M & Roseveare, A 2005a *Archaeological geophysical survey on the route of the N854 Luimneagh Realignment.* Unpublished report by ArchaeoPhysica Ltd for Galway County Council.

Roseveare, M & Roseveare, A 2005b *Archaeological geophysical survey on the route of the N17 Tuam Bypass.* Unpublished report by ArchaeoPhysica Ltd for Galway County Council.

Ryan, M 1973 'Native pottery in early historic Ireland', *Proceedings of the Royal Irish Academy,* Vol. 73C, 619–45.

Rynne, C 2006 *Industrial Ireland, 1750–1930: an archaeology.* Collins Press, Cork.

Schleifer, N 2004 'Ghost ridges', *ISAP News,* No. 1, 6–8.

Seaver, M 2006 'Through the mill—excavation of an early medieval settlement at Raystown, County Meath', *in* J O'Sullivan & M Stanley (eds), *Settlement, Industry and Ritual,* 73–87. Archaeology and the National Roads Authority Monograph Series No. 3. National Roads Authority, Dublin.

Sexton, R 1998 'Porridges, gruels and breads: the cereal foodstuffs of early medieval Ireland', *in* M Monk & J Sheehan (eds), *Early Medieval Munster: archaeology, history and society,* 76–86. Cork University Press, Cork.

Shaw, C 2003 *Butser Ancient Farm* (http://www.butser.org.uk/iafsoc_hcc.html, accessed November 2008).

Sherlock, R 2006 'Mural domestic bread ovens: evidence for the medieval–post-medieval architectural transition in County Cork', *Journal of the Cork Historical and Archaeological Society*, Vol. 111, 107–24.

Sheridan, A   1995 'Irish Neolithic pottery: the story in 1995', *in* I Kinnes & G Varndell (eds), *Unbaked Urns of Rudely Shape: essays on British and Irish pottery for Ian Longworth*, 3–21. Oxbow Monograph Series 55. Oxbow, Oxford.

Sheridan, A   2005 'Pitfalls and other traps—why it's worth looking at museum artefacts again', *The Archaeologist*, No. 58, 20–1.

Simpson, L   1999 *Director's Findings: Temple Bar West*. Temple Bar Archaeological Report No. 5. Temple Bar Properties, Dublin.

Smith, A   1852/3 'Kilkenny Tradesmen's Tokens', *Transactions of the Kilkenny Archaeological Society*, Vol. 2, 155–8.

Smyth, J   2006 'The role of the house in Early Neolithic Ireland', *European Journal of Archaeology*, Vol. 9, No. 2, 229–57.

Soderberg, J   2004 'Wild Cattle: red deer in the religious texts, iconography and archaeology of early medieval Ireland', *International Journal of Historical Archaeology*, Vol. 8, No. 3, 167–83.

Sparrow, J   2005 *Wild Brews: beer beyond the influence of brewer's yeast*. Brewers Publications, Boulder.

Stephens, D & Dudley, R   2004 'The drunken monkey hypothesis: the study of fruit-eating animals could lead to an evolutionary understanding of human alcohol abuse', *Natural History*, Vol. 113, No. 10, 40–4.

Stephens, K   1996 *Deer Hunting in Ireland from Prehistoric to Early Christian Times*. Unpublished MA thesis, University College Dublin.

Sternke, F   2008 *Lithics finds report for E2581 Busherstown, Co. Carlow*. Unpublished report for Headland Archaeology Ltd.

Stewart, K   2008a *N9/N10 Kilcullen to Waterford Scheme: Kilcullen to Powerstown. Archaeological Services Contract No. 4 Resolution, Prumpelstown to Powerstown, Palaeoenvironmental samples assessment for site E2571 Russellstown, Co. Carlow*. Unpublished report for Headland Archaeology Ltd.

Stewart, K   2008b *N9/N10 Kilcullen to Waterford Scheme: Kilcullen to Powerstown. Archaeological Services Contract No. 4 Resolution, Prumpelstown to Powerstown, Palaeoenvironmental samples assessment for site E2581 Busherstown, Co. Carlow*. Unpublished report for Headland Archaeology Ltd.

Stout, G & Stout, M   2008 *Excavation of a Secular Cemetery at Knowth Site M, County Meath, and Related Sites in North-east Leinster*. Wordwell, Dublin.

Stout, M   1997 *The Irish Ringfort*. Four Courts Press, Dublin.

Stuiver, M & Reimer, P J   1993 'Extended ^{14}C data base and revised CALIB 3.0 ^{14}C age calibration program', *Radiocarbon*, Vol. 35, No. 1, 215–30.

Stuiver, M, Reimer, P J, Bard, E et al.   1998 'IntCal98 Radiocarbon Age Calibration, 24,000–0 cal BP', *Radiocarbon*, Vol. 40, No. 3, 1041–83.

Stuiver, M, Reimer, P J & Reimer, R W   2005 *CALIB 5.0* (http://www.calib.qub.ac.uk/calib/).

Sweetman, H S & Handcock, G F   1886 *Calendar of Documents relating to Ireland, Preserved in Her Majesty's Public Record Office, London, Vol. 5, 1171–1307*. Longman, London.

Talma, A S & Vogel, J C   1993 'A simplified approach to calibrating ^{14}C dates', *Radiocarbon*, Vol. 35, No. 2, 317–32.

Taylor, A 1783 *Map of County Kildare.* Local Studies, Genealogy and Archives Department, Kildare Library and Arts Service, Newbridge.

Topping, P 1996 'Structure and ritual in the Neolithic house: some examples from Britain and Ireland', *in* T Darvill & J Thomas (eds), *Neolithic Houses of Northwest Europe and Beyond*, 157–70. Oxbow Books, Oxford.

Tourunen, A 2008 *Animals in an Urban Context. A Zooarchaeological Study of the Medieval and Post-Medieval town of Turku.* Annales Universitatis Turkuensis Ser B, Humaniora 308 (https://oa.doria.fi/handle/10024/36630, accessed November 2008).

Townshend, Rev. H 1810 *Statistical Survey of the County of Cork with Observations on the Means of Improvement.* Royal Dublin Society, Dublin.

van der Veen, M 1989 'Charred grain assemblage from Roman-period corn driers in Britain', *Archaeological Journal,* Vol. 146, 302–19.

van der Veen, M 2003 'When is food a luxury?', *World Archaeology,* Vol. 34, No. 3, 405–27.

van der Veen, M & Jones, G 2006 'A re-analysis of agricultural production and consumption: implications for understanding of the British Iron Age', *Vegetation History and Archaeobotany,* Vol. 15, No. 3, 217–28.

Walsh, F 2006 'Neolithic Monanny, County Monaghan', *in* J O'Sullivan & M Stanley (eds), *Settlement, Industry and Ritual*, 7–17. Archaeology and the National Roads Authority Monograph Series No. 3. National Roads Authority, Dublin.

Walsh, F 2007 'Tracing the Bronze Age in Tober', *Seanda*, No. 2, 14–15.

Ward, C L 2006 'Norse Drinking Traditions' (www.vikinganswerlady.com/resume/worksamples/NorseDrinkingTraditions.pdf, accessed November 2008).

Waterman, D M 1972 'A group of raths at Ballypalady, Co. Antrim', *Ulster Journal of Archaeology,* Vol. 35, 29–36.

Whitehouse, N J, McClatchie, M, Barratt, P, Schulting, R, Bogaard, A, Colledge, S, Reimer, P J, Marchant, R & McLaughlin, R (in prep.) 'A review of Irish Neolithic agriculture: new perspectives on agriculture, landscape and environment', *Antiquity.*

Young, A 1776–9 *A Tour in Ireland* (ed. H Morely, 1897). London, Paris, New York & Melbourne.